Twayne's English Authors Series

Sylvia E. Bowman, *Editor*

INDIANA UNIVERSITY

Max Beerbohm

TEAS 111

Max Beerbohm

by BRUCE R. McELDERRY, Jr.
University of Southern California

Twayne Publishers, Inc. :: New York

Library of Congress Catalog Card Number: 70-125257

MANUFACTURED IN THE UNITED STATES OF AMERICA

For Frances

Preface

From 1895 until his death in 1956, Max Beerbohm was known and relished wherever wit and choice English were appreciated. Several excellent books about him have appeared: Bohun Lynch's appreciative sketch; J. G. Riewald's elaborate bio-bibliography; S. N. Behrman's delightful account of his conversations with Max; and David Cecil's authoritative biography. All of these were written, quite appropriately, for an inner circle of readers already familiar with the essays, parodies, caricatures—and *Zuleika Dobson*. My book has profited from these and other writers on Beerbohm, but it differs from them in that it takes little for granted. For the reader who has seen a caricature or come upon a diverting quotation from Max, I seek to answer the unspoken question: who was Max Beerbohm? He was a man of such varied and unusual talents that his career is bound to interest many who know little or nothing about him. I have described that career as clearly and concisely as I could, emphasizing the energy that lay back of the idler's pose as a young man, the productiveness of the early years of retirement, his later withdrawal, and his re-emergence as a radio personality. His writings are described in sufficient detail to guide the reader in making further acquaintance with one of the best stylists of the twentieth century. The caricatures have been treated more selectively, with special emphasis on the captions which make the drawings literature as well as graphic art.

Though I have depended chiefly on published material, it has been my pleasure to consult during the preparation of this book the collections of Beerbohmiana at Charterhouse, Beerbohm's old school; at Merton College, Oxford; at the Ashmolean Museum, Oxford; at the Houghton Library, Harvard University; and in the Berg Collection, New York Public Library. Closer home, the resources of the Huntington Library, the William Andrews Clark Library of the University of California at Los Angeles, and the Library of the University of Southern California at Los Angeles have been available. Of the unpublished material

I have seen, I would say that it deepens rather than challenges the impressions made by Beerbohm's published writings, and by what has long been known of his career. I regret, however, that space did not pemit inclusion of some of the unpublished letters.

Thanks are due to the staffs of the libraries mentioned above. It is a pleasure to acknowledge once again assistance from the publications fund of the University of Southern California for supplying various research materials. My wife has shared my interest in Max and, at various stages, has given the manuscript of this book helpful criticism.

I am especially indebted to Sir Rupert Hart-Davis. His editions of Beerbohm's letters to Reggie Turner and of Oscar Wilde's letters, his projected editions of Beerbohm's uncollected essays, and his catalogue of Beerbohm's drawings, now in preparation, have given him a deep and precise knowledge of the period. He has kindly answered many questions and passed on information not generally accessible. His careful reading of my manuscript has enabled me to correct numerous errors, though of course I am responsible for any that remain.

For general permission to quote from the writings of Sir Max Beerbohm, I am indebted to Mrs. Eva Reichmann, and to her representative, Sir Rupert Hart-Davis. Thanks are due also to the following publishers for permission to quote from specific works in which they hold copyright: The Bodley Head, London, for *Works* (1896) and *More;* Dodd, Mead and Co., New York, for *Zuleika Dobson;* E. P. Dutton and Co., Inc., New York, for *A Christmas Garland* and *And Even Now,* Paperback edition (1960); Rupert Hart-Davis, Ltd., London, for *Around Theatres, Max's Nineties,* and *Max Beerbohm's Letters to Reggie Turner*; William Heinemann, Ltd., London, for *Seven Men, A Survey, Rossetti and His Circle, A Variety of Things,* and for the Beerbohm letter published by Bohun Lynch in *Max in Perspective;* Alfred A. Knopf, Inc., New York, for *Mainly on the Air* (1958); Simon & Schuster, Inc., for *Around Theatres* (American rights). The Washington State University Press has kindly permitted me to use passages from my essay, "Max Beerbohm: Essayist, Caricaturist, and Novelist," published in a volume entitled *On Stage and Off,* presented to my friend Emmett L. Avery.

Bruce R. McElderry, Jr.

University of Southern California

Contents

Chronology

1872 Henry Maximilian Beerbohm born at 57 Palace Gardens Terrace, Kensington, August 24. Youngest of nine children born to Julius Ewald Edward Beerbohm; fifth child of Julius's second wife, Eliza Draper Beerbohm.

1881–1885 Attended Mr. Wilkinson's day school, Orme Square.

1885–1890 Attended Charterhouse, Godalming, Sussex.

1890–1894 Merton College, Oxford. Left without taking a degree.

1892 Father died August 30. Published a series of caricatures in *The Strand.*

1893 Contributed to *The Spirit Lamp* at Oxford. Met William Rothenstein. Infatuation with Cissy Loftus, an actress. Autumn term in London.

1894 Contributed caricatures and essays to various publications, including *The Yellow Book.*

1895 Toured in America, January to April, with the theatrical company of his half-brother, Herbert Beerbohm Tree. Infatuation with Grace ("Kilseen") Conover began. First contribution to *The Saturday Review,* September.

1896 Published *The Works of Max Beerbohm,* June; *Caricatures of Twenty-five Gentlemen,* December. Began series of articles for *The Daily Mail,* December.

1898 Succeeded George Bernard Shaw as dramatic critic for *The Saturday Review,* May 28.

1899 Published *More,* a collection of essays, April.

1901 First exhibition of caricatures, Carfax Gallery, London, November.

1902 Infatuation with Constance Collier began.

1904 Second exhibition, Carfax Gallery, including drawings for *The Poets' Corner,* published in May. Met Florence Kahn.

1907 Third exhibition, Carfax Gallery, April. Published *A Book of Caricatures,* November.

1908 Fourth Exhibition, Carfax Gallery, April and May.

1909 Published *Yet Again,* a book of essays, October.

1910 Published last dramatic criticism in *The Saturday Review,* March 26. Married Florence Kahn, May 4. Settled in Rapallo, Italy, July.

1911 Exhibition of drawings at the Leicester Galleries, London, April and May. (Except as noted, all later exhibitions were at the Leicester Galleries.) Published *Zuleika Dobson,* October. Published *Cartoons,* drawings exhibited in 1901 at the time of the Boer War, December.

1912 Published *A Christmas Garland,* series of parodies, October.

1913 Exhibition of drawings, April and May. Published *Fifty Caricatures,* October.

1915–1919 Lived in England during World War I.

1919 Published *Seven Men,* October.

1920 Edited and published *Herbert Beerbohm Tree: Some Memories of His Art,* October; and *And Even Now,* a collection of essays, December.

1921 "Rossetti and His Circle" drawings exhibited, September. Published *A Survey,* caricatures, December.

1922–1928 Published *Works* in ten volumes.

1922 Published *Rossetti and His Circle,* September.

1923 Exhibition of drawings, June; public criticism of several portraying the royal family led Beerbohm to withdraw them. Published *Things New and Old,* caricatures, October.

1924 Published *Around Theatres,* a selection of his dramatic criticism, October.

1925 Exhibition of drawings, April–May. Published *Observations,* last important collection of caricatures, October.

1927 At Rapallo met Elisabeth Jungmann, then secretary to Gerhart Hauptmann.

1928 Published *A Variety of Things,* June. Exhibition entitled "Ghosts," including drawings of one hundred and nine persons Beerbohm had known, December.

1930 Honorary doctorate conferred by the University of Edinburgh.

1931 Published *Heroes and Heroines of Bitter Sweet*, five drawings of characters in Noel Coward's play.
1935 Return to England because war threatened.
1936–1938 At Rapallo.
1938–1947 In England.
1939 Knighted: honors published in June; ceremony July 13.
1942 Maximilian Society formed in honor of his seventieth birthday.
1943 Published *Lytton Strachey*, June, delivered earlier that year at Cambridge as the Rede Lecture.
1944 Exhibition at the Grolier Club, New York, September.
1945 Awarded honorary fellowship at Merton College, Oxford. Exhibition of caricatures owned by Philip Guedalla, September–October.
1946 Published *Mainly on the Air*, a collection of six radio talks and six "other things," September.
1947 Return to Rapallo, September. Exhibition of drawings, December.
1951 Florence, Lady Beerbohm, died January 13. Elisabeth Jungmann becomes Beerbohm's companion and nurse.
1952 Exhibition, "Max in Retrospect," May. Exhibition at the Academy Museum, New York, December-January. First of S. N. Behrman's visits.
1956 Beginning of final illness, March 10. Married Elisabeth Jungmann, April 20. Died May 20. Interment of ashes at Saint Paul's Cathedral, June 29.
1957 Memorial Exhibition, June.
1958 Enlarged edition of *Mainly on the Air*.

CHAPTER 1

Introduction: 1872-1894

THE career of Max Beerbohm was unique. Though he was born of a middle-class London merchant family, and proceeded in the normal way from day school to Charterhouse and thence to Oxford, he had established himself, even before he left the university, in the London circle of writers and painters as a young man to watch. This early fame—although helped by the prominence of his older half-brother, Herbert Beerbohm Tree, known to everyone as an important actor-manager—was mainly due to the talent and charm of young Max himself. His caricatures and essays appeared in magazines as popular as *The Strand* (then publishing the Sherlock Holmes stories) and as avant-garde as *The Yellow Book* and *The Savoy*. In 1898, when Beerbohm was not yet twenty-six, George Bernard Shaw welcomed him as his successor in reviewing plays for the influential *Saturday Review,* a post Beerbohm held until 1910. Meanwhile, he contributed occasional articles to other magazines and gathered his essays and caricatures into volumes that soon became collectors' items.

In 1910 Beerbohm married Florence Kahn, an American actress, and retired to a small house in Rapallo, Italy. There the Beerbohms lived quietly and happily until the death of Florence in 1951 and of Max in 1956. Max continued to write and draw at his leisure. From time to time he supervised exhibitions of his caricatures in London and planned in detail books that gathered together his writings and drawings. During both world wars the Beerbohms lived in England for several years; but, whether their visits were long or short, they always looked forward to returning to Italy. When old friends and celebrities sought them out in Rapallo, they were gracious hosts; but they preferred to be alone.

Beerbohm's retirement at thirty-eight has puzzled many people. Why, when most men are just achieving competence and influence, should so gifted a man, with a host of carefully selected friends, abandon London? Among many possible reasons, two are obvious. After twelve years, Max was tiring of the weekly stint of dramatic reviewing, and there was no clear alternative. A stronger reason was his marriage. Since Oxford days he had led a bachelor's life; his social position was that of a very charming, witty single man, eligible for the finest dinner parties without being obligated to give parties in return. He had not the money to maintain his social position as a married man. It was cheaper to live in Italy, and Florence was willing, even eager, to share life with him away from the brilliant friends who rather frightened her. Max seems never to have regretted the three interlocked decisions: to resign from *The Saturday Review,* to marry Florence, and to live in Italy.

From boyhood Max dressed as a dandy, and he affected the pose of the dilettante, the amateur in every pursuit, the man whose taste it is the business of others to please. There is truth in the pose, but not the whole truth. For a man of leisure, Max was extremely productive. When he died at eighty-three, he had published ten collections of caricatures, including about three hundred and fifty drawings; and in public and private collections over the world were some fourteen hundred additional drawings. There were also a dozen volumes of prose, including that extraordinary blend of fantasy and satire *Zuleika Dobson,* and *A Christmas Garland,* which established Beerbohm as one of the most successful parodists in English. His bibliographer has listed nearly five hundred uncollected pieces.

Beerbohm, the dramatic critic, tried his hand in five short plays, with some critical acclaim, though little profit. He even succeeded, when past sixty, at the new art of radio broadcasting. To those who listened to his first broadcast at the end of 1935, "London Revisited," and to those who heard him during and after World War II, Beerbohm was indeed a voice from the past —a living past when London was quieter and pleasanter, when music halls flourished, and when George Moore and William Butler Yeats were rising young men. To have achieved such diverse excellence, and to have known so effortlessly so many distinguished people along the way—Oscar Wilde, Aubrey Beardsley, George Bernard Shaw, Sir Arthur Pinero, John Galsworthy, Thomas Hardy, Henry James, H. G. Wells, Ramsay MacDonald, Lytton Strachey—required a great and peculiar energy. To describe and evaluate that energy is a main purpose of this book.

I *Childhood*

When Henry Maximilian Beerbohm was born, August 24, 1872,[1] his parents lived in a modest three-story house near the northwest corner of Kensington Gardens. By 1877 the family had moved not far away to Clanricarde Gardens, a short street north from Bayswater Road, with rather plain houses in a standardized row. This home he chiefly associated with his childhood. The boy's father, Julius Ewald Edward Beerbohm, was a grain merchant, with offices in the "City," four miles east; he also published a commercial paper. Julius Beerbohm, who had been born in Germany in 1810, had as a young man migrated first to France and then to London. In 1849 he married an English girl, Constantia Draper, who before her death in 1858 had borne him four children. Not long after her death, Julius married her sister, Eliza Draper. To this marriage were born four daughters and the one son, Henry Maximilian.

Little is known of either Mrs. Beerbohm. Max's mother welcomed his friends, and they appreciated her generous hospitality and her witty conversation. Somewhat impractical, she left the management of the household to her stepdaughter Constance. Max's father, punningly nicknamed "Superbe Homme" in Paris, was a cultivated man who spoke several languages, and it is curious that Max, in the many reminiscent passages in his writings, seldom speaks of him. The four children of the first marriage in particular showed diverse talents. Herbert, who was twenty years older than Max, had a remarkable career as actor and theater manager, and Constance achieved minor success as a writer of plays. Young Julius explored Patagonia, wrote a book about his adventures, and illustrated it himself. Max remembered Julius as a great dandy, full of money-making schemes which came to nothing. Ernest, the oldest son, went to Cape Colony to raise sheep.

Of the second family there were five children, of whom three survived. Marie Agnes was seven years older than Max; Dora Margaretta, four years older. Max, who felt particularly close to Dora, was sad when in 1893 she entered an Anglican order. Dora, however, retained her natural gaiety, and through letters and frequent family visits, and later visits to Rapallo, the association remained close. On her death in 1940, Max included in a brief but affectionate tribute a vivid glimpse of their nursery days. There was a trapeze on which Max liked to swing slowly, but Dora, he recalled, swung always "far and fast." [2] Dora was also involved, no doubt, in those parlor games he once recalled: "We had to amuse ourselves quietly, and tidily, or not at all." Rules of parlor games "gave us agony." English battles, he went on to say, were won not on the playing fields of Eton but on the drawing-room tables of Belgravia and Bayswater.[3]

Max's attachment to his older half-brother Herbert prompted other glimpses of his childhood. Under the name of Beerbohm Tree, Herbert was highly successful as an actor and as a theater manager from about 1878 until his death in 1917; he was knighted in 1907. In the memorial volume planned and edited by Max is a brief reminiscent sketch.[4] To the quiet little boy in Clanricarde Gardens, the handsome and buoyant Herbert represented the great world. While Max drew policemen he observed from his window, Herbert would produce sketches of James Whistler, the artist, or of Oscar Wilde, the poet, or of political figures like Disraeli and Gladstone. When Max was only nine, Herbert took him one Saturday morning to his own rooms, to the office of *Punch*, and to lunch at his club, introducing the boy to various celebrities. Forty years later Max could recall the thrill of that morning, particularly the ten-shilling gold piece Herbert gave him to pay his cab fare home. About this time Herbert began to bring his leading lady, Maud Holt, to the Beerbohms on Sunday afternoons. There she played and sang for the family. When Max was ten he was best man at the wedding of Herbert and Maud. During school and college days, and in the London years that followed, Max was a welcome guest at the Tree home. Max felt particularly close to the first daughter, Viola, born when Max was twelve.

Max's first schooling was delayed until 1881, when he was nine. For the next four years he attended Mr. Wilkinson's day school in Orme Square, a few blocks from the family home. There were only fifteen to twenty boys, and Mr. Wilkinson was the kind of schoolmaster who relished his pupils and their games, and encouraged whatever talents they had. Max showed an aptitude for Latin, and his drawing got direction from Mrs. Wilkinson, his only drawing teacher. Max's affection for Mr. Wilkinson was permanent, and years later they lunched together from time to time.

At twelve, Max's interest in drawing was stimulated when he pored over the photographs exhibited in a fashionable Regent Street shop window.[5] The Royal Family were there, the leading political figures, and other celebrities. On his way home the boy recognized a cabinet minister whose picture he had studied in the window. He did several drawings of this gentleman, and then took to haunting Number Ten Downing Street when Cabinet Council meetings were announced, so that he might watch these giants as they came and went. The following year he saw from the Strangers' Gallery in the House of Commons Gladstone himself (soon to become the prime minister for the third time). All during his childhood Max's interest in public figures was fed by the weekly issues of *Punch*. He describes how eagerly he looked forward to Wednesday mornings, when the magazine arrived with drawings by John Tenniel (illustrator of *Alice in Wonderland*), George du Maurier, and Charles Keene.[6]

II *Charterhouse*

Beerbohm, who went to Charterhouse in 1885 when he was thirteen, remained there until 1890. The school was originally founded in 1611 on the site of a Carthusian monastery in London. In 1872, the year Beerbohm was born, the school was moved to Godalming, Surrey, about thirty-five miles south of London. The buildings are on a high hill on the north side of the small town. An old archway, brought from London, reminded Beerbohm of such illustrious predecessors as Addison, Steele, John Leech (the *Punch* caricaturist), and Thackeray. The large library room, with its iron stove in the middle, is today much as it was in Beerbohm's time, when he was one of some four hundred schoolboys. The five years at Charterhouse were an unavoidable but not particularly attractive prelude to the freedom of the university. Later references to Charterhouse are humorous or mellowed by time, but never enthusiastic.

Ten years after leaving Charterhouse, Beerbohm saw a boy obviously on his way back to school after a holiday. "There but for the grace of God goes Max Beerbohm," he reflected, and he proceeded to write the essay "Going Back to School."[7] As the holidays drew to an end, he remembered counting the remaining hours at home and anticipating his departure with despair. He bought a first-class ticket so as to be alone on the train, and he walked slowly up the hill to the school buildings: "The awful geniality of the House Master! The jugs in the dormitory! . . . Next morning, the bell that awoke me!" He did not really hate school, he adds, but "in some respects I was always too young, in other too old, for a perfect relish of the convention."

As he thinks of the boy on his way to school, Beerbohm does not envy him his ordeals of construing Xenophon, memorizing Horace, mastering Euclid, and confronting a lockerful of tattered school books and heavy boots made for school wear. Addressing the boy, he predicts that tomorrow morning "you will have torn yourself from your bed, at the sound of a harsh bell, have washed, quickly, in very cold water, have scurried off to Chapel, gone to first school and been sent down several places in your form, tried to master your next construe, in the interval of snatching a tepid breakfast, been kicked by a bigger boy, and had a mint of horrible experiences. . . ."

In 1920, asked to contribute to the school paper, *The Carthusian*, Beerbohm expressed a softer view of his experience. "I was never a Carthusian of the straitest sect," he admits, especially since he never had any love for games. He left school not very proficient in French, algebra, and science; but he had been encouraged to progress in the things he did like, Latin prose and verse, and drawing caricatures. Looking back, he thinks he was not really happy at Charterhouse, as he later was at Oxford, and he dismisses the overworship of one's old school as sentimentality. Yet Charterhouse did teach him reasonably well to live with his fellows, and for this adjustment he is grateful.[8]

A picture of Max at Charterhouse shows a young dandy of perhaps sixteen.[9] He is dressed in the school costume of gray striped trousers, a dark jacket, and a waistcoat; he wears an unobtrusive watch chain and has a white handkerchief in the breast pocket. The right hand is nonchalantly stuck in his jacket pocket; the left hand holds a cane and top hat. The tie is enormous under the turn-down schoolboy collar. The round face looks even rounder with hair parted in the middle and plastered down. The expression is serious, self-possessed, and patrician. With this picture we may easily associate the boy's dislike of being a "fag," or servant, for older boys, and for having a fag when his age entitled him to one.[10] The picture, too, makes credible Beerbohm's story of how he ate a hamper full of sausage rolls alone, instead of sharing them with friends. He felt guilty, he says, but he ate the rolls with satisfaction.[11] Such seclusiveness and his dislike of games must have made the boy something of an oddity, but he was witty and could draw amusing caricatures of the masters. At Charterhouse, Beerbohm already knew how to be independent without being offensive.

Aside from school exercises, Beerbohm wrote little at Charterhouse. There is a satiric letter in the school paper inquiring of the editor, "Why this orthodox monotony?" There is the Latin poem "Carmen Becceriense," which one of the masters encouraged him to print; the English footnotes are amusing parodies of the academic manner: "Needless difficulties have been made over this line."[12] In his youth, and all his life, Beerbohm preferred drawing to writing. The masters, as well as the boys, relished his caricatures. The bewhiskered Dr. W. Haig Brown, then close to the end of his long career as headmaster, made an ideal subject. Beerbohm also drew his schoolmates as "Charterhouse Types" in exercise books, and he ornamented the minute book of the Charterhouse Society. He drew himself, projecting in one series various future careers: at Oxford, at the bar, and more prophetically at the Haymarket Theatre, not as actor, like Herbert, but as playgoer.[13]

We know little of Beerbohm's reading at this period. He mentions Walter Pater's *Marius the Epicurean* as a book that pleased him more than the standard adventure story of the day, Frederick Marryat's *Midshipman Easy*. Thackeray was an early and permanent favorite. Vacations at home stimulated interest in contemporary writers, for from the time he was fifteen he was frequently included in the after-theater parties given by Herbert. The social knowledge which many boys grope for painfully and awkwardly in libraries came to young Max as naturally as the air he breathed. For him, literature never had that separateness from life which is so dangerous to a sense of proportion.[14]

III *Oxford*

Beerbohm was eighteen when he entered Merton College, Oxford, in the autumn of 1890. His first letter home to his mother suggests that, despite his worldly knowledge, he was a little overawed.[15] He reported attending the college chapel on his first Sunday at eight-thirty and again at five in the afternoon. Unathletic as he was, Oxford stimulated him to consider going in for boating, though he did not actually pursue so strenuous an activity. In an essay written five years later,[16] he recalled, no doubt with some exaggeration, his disappointing first impressions. The town, he thought, looked like a bit of Manchester. Amid the trams, electric lights, and shouting newsboys, there were only remnants of Oxford's ancient beauty. Trains ran so frequently to London that Oxford was almost a suburb. The spirit of Oxford conjured up by the writings of Pater was inaccessible.

Within the walls of Merton, however, Oxford was still Oxford. For his first year Beerbohm lived in Mob Quad, that is, in the college quadrangle; thereafter, he had rooms at Number nineteen in quiet little Merton Street. In 1890 Merton College had ninety men, not many more than the sixth form at Charterhouse. Even in this small group Beerbohm was selective in his friendships, for a year or so later he was complaining that Merton men he scarcely knew tried to seek him out in London during holidays.[17] Of the Myrmidons, a college club, Beerbohm later wrote an essay in which he speaks of bonfires in the quadrangle, of smashed windows, and of "unlimited loo" (a card game). Another club, *Septem Contra Somnum* (Seven against Sleep), eventually merged with the Myrmidons.[18] Elsewhere Beerbohm recalls a little "Essay Society," in which an overeager member tried in vain to rouse enthusiasm for Giuseppe Mazzini, the Italian liberator.[19] To his mother, Max reported his great success in this society when he spoke on the theater.[20]

Beerbohm met men outside Merton, of course. An early acquaintance was H. B. Irving of New College, son of the great Shakespearean actor. What Irving thought of Beerbohm is hard to discover, but Beerbohm remembered saying quietly to many acquaintances that day in 1890, "I met young Irving at breakfast this morning."[21] Beerbohm's own fame spread, partly because of his wit and partly through the display of his caricatures at Shrimpton's, a familiar print shop. In 1893 there is reference to a dinner at which Lord Alfred Douglas and several friends from various colleges were present. Douglas, a friend of Wilde, soon involved Beerbohm in a literary magazine called *The Spirit Lamp.*

In the summer of 1893 Beerbohm, in a letter to a friend, summed up the pleasures of Oxford: "To dress carefully, to lie in a canoe in the summer and read minor verse by the fire in the winter, to talk of Oscar [Wilde], to sit down to dinner looking forward to rising from it drunk, to draw more or less amusing caricatures—a few friends, a few theatres and music halls and a few cigarettes a day—and there you have my life."[22] It was thus that the nonsense knocked out of young Beerbohm at Charterhouse was "gently put back" at Oxford: "I was a modest, good-humoured boy. It is Oxford that has made me insufferable."[23]

Dons and studies did exist, of course. There was G. R. Scott, his first tutor, who laughed when the young freshman expressed a desire to attend the lectures of Pater. There were Thomas Bowman, chief disciplinarian at Merton, whom Beerbohm gaily caricatured; ponderous George Brodrick, Warden of the college; Dr. William Walter Merry, whose summer lectures on Aristophanes Beerbohm recalled with pleasure when he reviewed the Oxford Union Dramatic Society production of *The Clouds.*[24] In the legendary background was Dr. Benjamin Jowett, "the Jowler," famed translator of Plato; Beerbohm thought it worth recording that he once saw Jowett ride by in a carriage. As to his own studies, Beerbohm in 1892 took a third class in Greek and Latin ("Moderations," as the examinations were called), hardly a distinguished showing. At the end of his third year, he seriously considered taking a pass degree and leaving Oxford. Persuaded to stay and read for Honours, partly because he would be permitted to study in London during the autumn term, he stayed on until June, 1894; but, since he did not take the examinations, he left without a degree. There is no hint that lack of a degree was ever a source of regret.

As the years went by, a golden haze settled over his image of Oxford. He welcomed opportunities to review productions of the Oxford Union Dramatic Society (OUDS), and he was uniformly kind to these amateur efforts. In his reviews he liked to include some general commendation of Oxford itself, as when he wrote in 1901: "Oxford was at its very best last week, with the candles of its vast horse-chestnuts still alight and unshamed by the imperious sun, and with its lilac and laburnum still a-wave to mock the staid gravity and grayness of its walls." In 1903 he expressed the Tory spirit of the place: "Let us spare Oxford. Let us keep it, that dear place, if only as a curiosity, a relic of dark ages. It need do no harm." The brightest youth, he playfully suggests, could be sent to the University of Birmingham instead. In 1907 he proclaimed: "Oxford's business is to 'sit tight'." And in 1908 he summed up the Oxford spirit: "Oxford teaches you to seem not to commit yourself, not to unbosom yourself, to be gently aloof."[25]

That Oxford that Beerbohm chiefly knew from 1890 to 1894 was a playground of privilege, a social club that remained relatively unchanged from 1850 to 1914. The affectations, social and academic, he was later to satirize brilliantly in *Zuleika Dobson*. The genuine good fellowship, the peculiar blend of good form and wide tolerances, gaiety and good sense, Beerbohm treasured for the rest of his life. There was, however, much of Oxford that passed him by. In 1888 Mrs. Humphry Ward published *Robert Elsmere*, a novel about a young Oxonian who entered the church; became preoccupied with liberal theology; and eventually, for reasons of conscience, gave up his calling as priest. This novel, which drew personal attention from Gladstone and in twenty years sold a million copies, reflected the serious Oxford which co-existed with the country club. Though Beerbohm occasionally alludes to Matthew Arnold, uncle of Mrs. Humphry Ward, the Oxford of lost causes had little impact on Beerbohm or his friends.

IV *Turner and Rothenstein*

Two of Beerbohm's friends during the Oxford years were also close links with the life he lived in London during holidays—the life to which he returned so eagerly when university days were over. The fusion of school and college with the "real" world is indeed a major reason for Beerbohm's early success as writer and caricaturist. Among his Oxford-London friends was Reggie Turner, who was in his third year at Merton when Beerbohm arrived in 1890; Beerbohm's first letter to him indicates that they had become close friends in Max's first year. In 1892 Turner took his degree and went to London to read for the bar, but the friendship continued through frequent meetings and letters until Turner's death in Italy in 1938. In the early years, Max was eager that Turner have copies of everything he wrote; and Turner's own superficial society novels were always acknowledged with praise. Though Turner's novels were thin, he shone in conversation. Beerbohm considered him one of the best talkers he had ever known.[26]

Less intimate as personal friend in the Oxford years than Turner, but even more important intellectually and artistically was William Rothenstein, the young artist whom Beerbohm met in the summer of 1893. After leaving school in Yorkshire, Rothenstein had gone to the Slade School of Art in London and then spent several years in Paris. At twenty-one, exactly Beerbohm's age, he was already acquainted with Wilde and Whistler; and when he visited Oxford to do a series of sketches of university celebrities, Rothenstein discovered old schoolmates and quickly made his way into Oxford society. In the semifictional "Enoch Soames," written twenty years later, Beerbohm describes their meeting:

> In the summer of '93 a bolt from the blue flashed down upon Oxford. . . . Its name? Will Rothenstein. Its aim? To do a series of twenty-four portraits in lithograph. These were to be published from the Bodley Head [John Lane's company], London. . . . He was twenty-one years old. He wore spectacles that flashed more than any other pair ever seen. He was a wit. He was brimful of ideas. He knew Whistler. He knew Edmond de Goncourt. He knew everyone in Paris. He knew them all by heart. He was Paris in Oxford.[27]

Rothenstein's impression of Beerbohm is even more circumstantial:

> A baby face, with heavily lidded, very light grey eyes shaded by remarkably thick and long lashes, a broad forehead, and sleek black hair parted in the middle and coming to a queer curling point at the neck; a quiet and finished manner; rather tall, carefully dressed; slender fingered, with an assurance and experience unusual in one of his years—I was at once drawn to Max Beerbohm and lost no time in responding to an invitation to breakfast. He was living in a tiny house at the end of Merton Street—a house hardly bigger than a Punch and Judy show. His room, blue-papered, was hung with Pellegrini prints from *Vanity Fair* [caricatures by "Ape"]. Besides these, there were some amusing caricatures which, he said modestly, were his own. "But they are brilliant," I said, and he seemed pleased at my liking them.[28]

Rothenstein's drawing of Beerbohm, included in *Oxford Characters* (1896),[29] does indeed show a self-assured young man, with tall collar and a variant of the flowing windsor tie. When Rothenstein returned to London, he sang the praises of the brilliant young Merton undergraduate. Since Beerbohm spent the autumn term of 1893 in London, ostensibly for study, Rothenstein was able to introduce him to Aubrey Beardsley, Walter Sickert, and other artists. Rothenstein also introduced him to John Lane, later the publisher of *The Yellow Book.* The friendship remained close, as the numerous letters in Rothenstein's memoirs show. When Rothenstein died in 1945, Beerbohm delivered the memorial address.

V *Oscar Wilde*

Another friend of the Oxford period, well known to Reggie Turner and to Rothenstein, was Oscar Wilde. It was through Herbert Beerbohm Tree that Max first came to know him, at a supper party in 1889 when Max was still at Charterhouse, and more importantly in the spring of 1893 when Herbert was producing Wilde's *A Woman of No Importance.*[30] At the same time, Wilde was frequently in Oxford, drawn there by Lord Alfred Douglas, whom Max knew.

Wilde, then thirty-seven, was at the height of his fame. Influenced by Ruskin and Pater, he had adopted and popularized —even vulgarized—the esthetic approach to life which they had commended. Despite Wilde's languid pose and his announced intention to live up to his blue china, he had had a brilliant record at Magdalen College, Oxford, and he was a celebrity when he took his degree in 1878. His exotic clothes (knee breeches and velvet jackets on occasion), his witty rejection of middle-class morality ("There is no sin except stupidity"), and the excessive emotion of his poems soon made him a favorite target of *Punch.* In 1881 Wilde was easily recognizable as the young man in Gilbert and Sullivan's very popular *Patience*[31] "who strolled down Piccadilly with a lily in his hand." A lecture tour in America in 1882 gave Wilde great notoriety, and after his return to London he remained the most talked-about literary man. Then came the notable series of plays: *Salomé,* published in 1893 after presentation was prohibited in 1892; *A Woman of No Importance* and *Lady Windemere's Fan,* 1893; *The Ideal*

Husband and *The Importance of Being Earnest,* 1895. Meanwhile, *The Picture of Dorian Gray* (1891), a decadent story of a man obsessed with evil, created a sensation.

In 1895, when two of his plays were running in London, Wilde was accused of homosexuality by the Marquis of Queensberry, father of Lord Alfred Douglas, a close associate of Wilde, and well known to Beerbohm, Turner, and Rothenstein. At the end of three complex and interlocking court cases, Wilde was convicted of "acts of gross indecency" and sentenced to two years at hard labor. On his release, he went to France; he died in Paris late in 1900.

Beerbohm, who enjoyed Wilde's wit, speaks of him in 1893 with friendly affection. In August, 1894, he mentions lunching with Wilde and "Bosie" (Lord Alfred Douglas) in London: "Oscar was just in the mood that I like him—very 1880 and withal brimful of intellectual theories and anecdotes of Dear Lady Dorothy Nevill and other whores." Yet the previous year Beerbohm had had some misgivings: "I am sorry to say that Oscar drinks far more than he ought: indeed the first time I saw him, after all that long period of distant adoration and reverence, he was in a hopeless state of intoxication. He has deteriorated much in appearance: his cheeks being quite a dark purple and fat to a fault." [32]

Beerbohm's acquaintance with Wilde prompted numerous caricatures, most of them exaggerating the swirl of Wilde's luxuriant hair, his extravagant cravats, and his considerable girth—a curious combination of foppishness and grossness. Beerbohm, once told of Wilde's displeasure at one of his caricatures, wrote with surprising vigor to Turner: "How I wish he had written me on the subject and how I could have crushed him." [33] As long as Wilde interested him, he said, he would go on drawing him; after all, Wilde was for him "simply an unpaid model." There are also two notable written accounts of Wilde by Beerbohm. One, only recently brought to light, was a brief article published in the *Anglo-American Times* and oddly captioned "Oscar Wilde by an American." [34] In letters to Turner, Beerbohm proudly reported that Wilde himself had praised the article as an extraordinary production for an undergraduate. The article gives a vivid description of Wilde, with numerous anecdotes and witticisms. Since the tone is that of conventional eulogy, with none of

Beerbohm's characteristic irony, it is no wonder that Wilde enjoyed it.

A Peep into the Past,[35] said to have been written for the first number of *The Yellow Book* (April, 1894), is, in contrast to the article, a small masterpiece of parody. It purports to be an interview with an aged Oscar Wilde, now forgotten by the general public. "He lives now in retirement in his little house in Tite Street," Beerbohm reports. Wilde solaces himself with the classics, Keats, Shakespeare, Joseph Miller (author of the famous jest book), and the Greek dramatists. The juxtaposition of Joseph Miller, with its suggestion that Wilde's famous wit was often borrowed, is a very sly touch. Wilde, it is said, is now an early riser; at four-thirty each morning, he boils his own cup of hot cocoa. Toward the end of the interview, Wilde tells a familiar Whistler story as if it were new. At signs of a storm, Wilde remarks, "Ah, yes, I expect we shall soon *see* the thunder and *hear* the lightning!" The essay concludes: "I left the old gentleman chuckling immoderately at his little joke." *A Peep into the Past,* more explicitly than the well-known caricatures, states Beerbohm's reservations about Wilde. It anticipates the parodies of other writers in *A Christmas Garland* (1912), and it is altogether a remarkable production for a young man of twenty-one or twenty-two. It is characteristic of Beerbohm that, after the Wilde scandal, he himself never published the imagined interview. Unauthorized publication in America angered him and perhaps led him to underrate its quality.

The scandal broke in the spring of 1895, while Beerbohm was touring America with his brother's theatrical company. In February the Marquis of Queensberry left a card at Wilde's club, accusing him of "posing" as a sodomite. Wilde decided to prefer charges on the ground of criminal libel, and Queensberry was arrested on April 1. In the three-day trial Wilde was forced to make damaging admissions which resulted in the acquittal of Queensberry and in the arrest of Wilde himself on the same day. He was imprisoned without bail until the trial, which, despite sensational evidence by male prostitutes, ended in disagreement of the jury. Meanwhile, Mrs. Wilde, appalled by the disaster, had taken her two sons away from the house in Tite Street, Chelsea, and on April 24 creditors auctioned off the books and furnishings. On May 7 Wilde was released on bail of five thousand pounds, but he obstinately refused to take the advice of friends to leave the country. A new trial began on May 20, and on May 25 he was sentenced to prison for two years. After six months at Wandsworth, he was transferred to the Reading Gaol of his famous ballad. When he was released on March 19, 1897, Reggie Turner was one of the two friends who accompanied him to Dieppe; three years later, when Wilde died in Paris, Turner was one of the two friends who attended him. The other friend, on both occasions, was Robert Ross, art critic, and Wilde's literary executor.

Beerbohm's attitude toward Wilde before and after the scandal is puzzling. That he knew of Wilde's homosexuality is evident from a jocular reference to Oscar's arrest "for certain kinds of crime" in a letter to Turner in August, 1894. Prophetic as it was, the phrase seems a poor joke. When, in America, Beerbohm first heard the news of Wilde's suit against Queensberry, he exclaimed in a letter to Turner: "Poor, poor Oscar! How very sad it is." Returning to London a few weeks later, Beerbohm attended the second trial (the first one in which Wilde himself faced charges), and reported to Turner, then in Europe: "Oscar was quite superb. His speech about the Love that dares not tell his name was simply wonderful, and carried the whole court right away, quite a tremendous burst of applause." The night before this trial began, Beerbohm was with the Leversons, staunch friends of Wilde. Douglas, also there, was ready to leave for France at the urgent request of Wilde's lawyers. Apparently, however, Beerbohm had no contact with Wilde himself during the trials or during his imprisonment; but, prior to Wilde's release, Beerbohm sent him several books, for which Wilde wrote his thanks.

On the news of Wilde's death, late in 1900, Beerbohm wrote to Turner: "I am, as you may imagine, very sorry indeed; and am thinking very much about Oscar, who was such an influence and an interest in my life. Will you please lay out a little money for me in flowers for the grave?" He added that he hoped to write something nice about Oscar in his next *Saturday Review* article. "Of course," he noted, "I shall have to ask Hodge [the editor] first, whether he has any objection." The comment, which duly appeared as a long paragraph appended to the review of a play by Louis N. Parker, December 8, 1900, is wholly a tribute to Wilde's talent as a playwright.[36]

The record is thus ambiguous. If Beerbohm did not join the chorus of condemnation, he did not clearly or boldly align himself with Wilde's defenders. In the spring of 1895 Beerbohm was not quite twenty-three. Though he had considerable tolerance for homosexuality among his friends, as his association with Wilde, Douglas, Ross, and Turner shows, he probably recognized on practical grounds that the public outcry could not be effectively opposed. His revulsion at the male prostitutes that crowded around the courtroom indicates a disapproval on grounds of taste. The failure to see Wilde in prison or after his release—it would surely have been safe enough to do so in France—is perhaps explainable also on grounds of taste. Beerbohm was genuinely sorry for Wilde, but Wilde was no longer the man he had known in 1893 and 1894. Beerbohm's attitude was not a courageous one, nor one of deep human sympathy; but it was shared by many of Wilde's old associates.

A well-known critic has recently stated, without evidence, that Beerbohm himself was a homosexual. It is doubtful whether any evidence exists except through the discredited device of "guilt by association." A letter to Robert Ross, kindly suggesting that Ross not see too much of Turner, shows Beerbohm's concern to curb Turner's inclination. In 1906, when in Florence, Italy, Beerbohm stayed in rooms formerly occupied by Turner; writing to his friend, Beerbohm comments on the small painted faces in the ceiling "which have, I feel, looked down on scenes which I should not have approved of." These trifling details, which by no means "prove" anything, fit well, however, with the theory that Beerbohm's relations with men, as well as women, were little tinged with sexual feeling.[37]

At the very time of Beerbohm's closest association with Wilde, he became infatuated with Cissie Loftus, a music-hall singer and mimic only fifteen years old. The letters to Turner in 1893 and 1894 speak effusively of her charms. A contemporary portrait shows a girlish face with serious expression, and loose brown hair falling over her shoulders.[38] Hat and dress are almost awkwardly plain. Beerbohm wrote to Turner: "to me she is a girl, an artist, a child from the convent, an exquisite thing." He deplored seeing her in the same room with cads and harlots. He suffered when he heard her sing suggestive songs he was sure she could not really understand. In September, 1893, he who was to write the following year "A Defence of Cosmetics" professed to be out of love with Cissie because she piled "a Pelion of rouge upon an Ossa of powder"; but a few days later he "grudged every evening" he could not spend in the music hall where she appeared. In 1894, when Cissie married Justin McCarthy, the dramatist and historian, Beerbohm showed no visible effects of disappointment. The whole tone of the affair was light and self-indulgent rather than serious. Since Dora, Beerbohm's favorite sister, entered an Anglican order in August, 1893, he may have seen in Cissie a substitute for her. It is clear, at any rate, that Cissie was a refreshing contrast to the corruption of Wilde and his group.

VI *The Literary Scene:* The Yellow Book

Although Oscar Wilde was the most conspicuous literary figure of the early 1890's, other talents were numerous. Rudyard Kipling, already established by his fiction, published *Barrack-Room Ballads* in 1892. Yeats's first volume of thinly romantic poems came in 1895, Housman's *Shropshire Lad* in 1896, and Hardy's *Wessex Poems* in 1898. Other poets of the period were William Ernest Henley, Fiona MacLeod (William Sharp), Ernest Dowson, and Francis Thompson. Besides the plays of Wilde, vigorous new drama came from Arthur Wing Pinero, Henry Arthur Jones, and George Bernard Shaw. Wilde's sensational novel was overshadowed by the later fiction of Henry James, George Meredith, and Thomas Hardy, as well as by the early novels of H. G. Wells and Joseph Conrad.

On a more popular level, three novels published in 1894 suggest the volatile mood of London in the year that Beerbohm left Oxford to begin his career as free-lance writer and caricaturist. Robert Hichens's *The Green Carnation* cleverly satirized Wilde as Esmé Amarinth, whose clique of young men admirers wear green carnations as a badge. The almost nonexistent plot leaves Esmé free to utter his Wildean epigrams. Operas, he thinks, should be given at noon, "to unfit one for the duties of the day." Duty, he says, is "like some horrible disease." A word that he detests is "natural": it suggests "all that is middle-class, all that is the essence of jingoism, all that is colorless, and without form, and void." [39]

A very different sort of novel was George Moore's *Esther Waters,* a story about a servant girl whose misfortunes illustrate over and over the cruelty and hypocrisy of the double standard in sex. George du Maurier's *Trilby* was an immensely popular romantic tale of three young English artists living in Paris about 1850. One of these young men falls hopelessly in love with Trilby, a model. In an effort to save her lover from what she knows will be a disastrous marriage for him, Trilby falls into the clutches of Svengali, whose hypnotic power turns Trilby into a famous concert singer. So popular was this farfetched novel that "Svengali" became a byword, and "Trilby" the name of a hat popular with romantic young women.

Against the background of such literary fads and fancies as *The Green Carnation, Esther Waters,* and *Trilby, The Yellow Book* had its brief success. Various stories of its origin have been told, but it is most likely that a conversation between Henry Harland and Aubrey Beardsley on New Year's Day, 1894, resulted in the plan.[40] The next day John Lane, publisher of "new" writing and a friend of Rothenstein, agreed to finance the magazine. Henry Harland, an American writer just over thirty, who had been living in London for some time, was literary editor. Aubrey Beardsley, who at twenty-two had already achieved fame by his illustrations of Malory's *Morte d'Arthur* (1893), was art editor. Almost immediately Beerbohm, who already knew Harland, Beardsley, and Lane, was asked to draw and write for the new magazine.

In March, a "Prospectus" appeared, with a Beardsley cover and an impressive "incomplete" list of fifteen artists and forty-four writers who had agreed to contribute. *The Yellow Book,* it was announced, would "seek always to preserve a delicate, decorous, and reticent mien and conduct"; but "it will at the same time have the courage of its modernness, and not tremble at the fear of Mrs. Grundy." In April, the first number appeared, substantially bound so that, although it was a quarterly periodical, each issue was to be thought of by the reader as a *book.* On the day of publication, newsstands were covered with the yellow of the first issue, and that night editors and contributors celebrated with a dinner.

The first issue included Henry James's "The Death of a Lion," poems by young Richard Le Gallienne and Edmund Gosse, two short plays, and several essays; the drawings were by Walter Sickert, Will Rothenstein, Joseph Pennell (disciple of Whistler), and even Sir Frederick Leighton of the Royal Academy. In such a context, Beerbohm's essay, "The Pervasion of Rouge," struck a different but not discordant note. "The Victorian era comes to its end," he announced, "and the day of sancta simplicitas is quite ended." "We are all gamblers once more," he continued; and, like the return of cosmetics, this fact is a great sign of "a more complicated life." The old following of nature has lately led women to invade tennis courts and golf links, to use bicycles and typewriters. This dangerous trend will be stopped by the use of artifice. "Too long," he said, "has the face been degraded from its rank as a thing of beauty to a mere vulgar index of character or emotion." These views were expanded with appropriate allusions to Ovid, a few French phrases, and a paradoxical tribute to Cissie Loftus. Yes, she had made her success by her girlish innocence, but such success was only possible because it challenged the convention of rouge behind the footlights. Besides, there was more artfulness in her performance than met the eye. He concluded: "Artifice, sweetest exile, is come unto her kingdom. Let us dance her a welcome." [41]

Punch, extending its ridicule of Wilde and the esthetic movement of the 1880's, alluded ponderously to the "stumious Beerbohmax" and the "Daycaydongs." Even the serious magazines greeted the first number of *The Yellow Book* with an alarm now amusing. *The Westminster Gazette* called for "an Act of Parliament to make this kind of thing illegal." [42] Beerbohm was specifically named as the only writer worthy to be ranked with the offensive Mr. Beardsley. All this publicity gave Beerbohm an opportunity to publish in the second issue a letter to the editor in which he assured the "affrightened mob" that it had completely missed his satirical intent.

In the October *Yellow Book* appeared Beerbohm's "A Note on George the Fourth," a refutation of Thackeray's famous derogatory lecture of 1860. Though Beerbohm says that Thackeray "applied to his subject the wrong method, in the wrong manner, at the wrong time," something of Thackeray's method is evident in the *Yellow Book* essay. The facts from the library are distilled into the idiom of the man of the world, with a purpose opposite from that of Thackeray. "How strange it must be to be a king!"

Beerbohm comments. "How delicate and difficult a task it is to judge him!" The present is a degenerate and feeble time; the age of George IV was vigorous, "full of life and color and wrong and revelry."

Such a society gave great license to a young prince who had been badly brought up and longed to be free of parental supervision. The affair with Mrs. Fitzherbert and the state marriage with Caroline show his weakness, but George deserves some pity in both affairs. The politics of the time forced him into unfortunate positions, and the fact that he was heir-apparent kept him out of the army against his own wish. His life, nevertheless, was "a poem in praise of pleasure." He was as fine a raconteur as Walter Scott, a patron of good painters, something of a scholar, and he set a tone for society, typified by the Pavilion at Brighton.[43]

Written when Beerbohm was only twenty-three, the essay on George IV shows a vivid sense of history, a flexible, mature style, and a humane restraint. Either Wilde or Shaw would have heaped abuse or contempt on Thackeray's denunciation of George IV. Instead, Beerbohm states his high opinion of Thackeray, though his style is now "somewhat 1860." Thackeray's lecture on George IV is treated as a regrettable lapse. Although Beerbohm's sophistication in defense of cosmetics in the April *Yellow Book* was largely counterfeit, a good piece of youthful foolery, the essay on George IV shows the real sophistication which was to be Beerbohm's great distinction: not a smartness of paradox, but a genuine superiority to prevailing opinion.

VII *Achievement to 1895*

When Beerbohm left Oxford in June, 1894, he returned to a familiar, pleasant pattern of life in London. About 1889 or 1890 the family had settled at 19 Hyde Park Place, not far from Marble Arch and near the theaters and art galleries. Across Hyde Park, which he enjoyed from the windows of his top-floor room, and a little to the west, lay Chelsea, where Wilde and many other friends lived. It was comfortable to live at home. Max's widowed mother and his sisters were witty conversationalists, and they extended a warm welcome to his friends. There was money enough so that Max felt no pressure to contribute to the household expenses. He was free to follow a routine of drawing and writing in his own room, and to dine out or go to the theater in the evening. When Herbert was in London, Max could visit him at home or at his club, the Garrick. It was a pleasant life, with little responsibility.

At the end of 1894 Beerbohm could regard his situation with some satisfaction. He had not taken a degree at Oxford, but among writers and artists in London this lack was no disadvantage. He had had the social experience of Charterhouse and Oxford, and he had gained an easy acquaintance with books and, more important, with many of his generation who would write the new ones. No one doubted his abilities. Exactly how he was to use them was not quite clear, but he had made a promising beginning as essayist and caricaturist.

As yet he had not written a great deal. Besides the two *Yellow Book* essays of 1894, he had contributed to Lord Alfred Douglas's *Spirit Lamp;* he had published an unsigned article on Wilde and had in manuscript *A Peep into the Past;* and he had published a lively interview with Oxford's great cricket player, "Fry of Wadham." A third *Yellow Book* essay was to appear in the issue of January, 1895.

Drawing came more easily than writing, and he had sold some of his work before he left Oxford. In 1892 one of his sisters showed some of his drawings to the editor of the *Strand.* The editor liked what he saw, and in September, October, and December appeared the series of thirty-six small drawings entitled "Club Types." Two years later the same magazine published an article, "Oxford at Home," illustrated by Beerbohm.[44] Meanwhile, between May and December, 1894, Beerbohm himself listed twenty-one caricatures in such popular magazines as *Sketch, Pall Mall, Budget,* and *Pick-Me-Up.* In the last publication, four other drawings appeared in January, 1895. The subjects were varied: the idolized Cissie Loftus, Herbert Tree, and Henry Irving represented the stage; Aubrey Beardsley and the cartoonist Phil May were well-known artists; and Arthur Balfour and Sir William Harcourt were prominent political figures.

When Beerbohm left England in January, 1895, for a few months in America with his brother's theatrical company, he was as free as a free lance could be, and he was open to new ideas and new experience. While absent from London, he could be sure that friends in editorial offices would eagerly await his return.

CHAPTER 2

The Active Years: 1895-1910

ON January 16, 1895, Herbert Beerbohm Tree's company sailed for America. Max went along as private secretary to Herbert; but, because he composed letters with such care that he got far behind, he was soon relieved of his duties; Herbert good-naturedly continued his salary. After six weeks in New York, the company later appeared in Chicago, Philadelphia, Boston, Baltimore, and Washington, D.C. On his arrival, Max found New York "too terrible" and planned a "slashing article" for *The Yellow Book.* A few weeks later, however, he reported to Turner that New York had given itself to him "like a flower." He even liked Chicago, despite "The vast and hideous debauchery" of a town-ball and visits to certain houses where "black women danced naked to the sound of the piano." While in Boston, Herbert was invited to give a Shakespeare reading at Harvard, and Max accompanied him. In Baltimore, Rudyard Kipling came backstage and on meeting Max expressed surprise at his youth; it was the only time Max met the writer whom he later satirized so often. In Washington, the company was taken to meet President Grover Cleveland amid guards and precautions that led Maud Tree to write a witty reminiscence.[1]

The slashing attack on New York and the parodies of Oscar Wilde's poems mentioned in the same letter seem never to have been written. Max did publish in the New York *Vanity* four articles on "Dandies and Dandies," reworked from his Oxford essay, "The Incomparable Beauty of Modern Dress"—"certain Oxford flies dipped in my American amber," as he said.[2] "De Natura Barbatulorum" ("Of Small Beards") appeared in the Chicago *Chap-Book* in February, 1896. These, with "Notes on Foppery" published in the London *Unicorn* (September 18 and 25, 1895) he reworked into "Dandies and Dandies," the first item in his collection, *Works* (1896). All these pieces are clearly in the Wildean esthetic vein, similar in tone to "The Perversion of Rouge" in the first issue of *The Yellow Book.*

Since drawing was always easier and pleasanter for Beerbohm than writing, it is strange that American personalities he encountered did not lead him to caricature them. The *Pick-Me-Up* series, begun in 1894, carried over into the spring with a total of thirty-one drawings, but they were wholly English in subject. Though he later married an American, and attracted many American readers, Beerbohm never again visited America.

I *Grace Conover and Constance Collier*

An important consequence of the tour in America was Beerbohm's acquaintance with one of the actresses, Grace Conover, a dark Irish girl of twenty. In a letter to Turner, Beerbohm describes a conversation with her as she peered out between the curtains of a sleeping car on the train to Chicago, looking, he said, extremely attractive in her nightgown. Thereafter the two spent much time together, and within a short time Beerbohm asked her to marry him. She was uncertain whether to take him seriously. He had, for instance, teased her by telling her that at the theater she was known as "Kill-scene Conover" because she killed every scene in which she appeared. The name stuck, and to Beerbohm and his friends she remained "Kilseen." Back in London, to which Beerbohm returned in late April, they continued to see each other for several years, though the Beerbohm family was not pleased with the association; his mother and sisters found Kilseen's voice unpleasant, her manner too common. However, Max was so great a favorite at home that probably any girl who threatened to take him away from the household would have aroused criticism. Kilseen's frequent visits created friction, and even Maud Tree, Herbert's wife, on one occasion angered Max into breaking off acquaintance with the Trees; eventually the quarrel was smoothed over. Beerbohm's "engagement" to Kilseen, never formally announced, continued until 1903 and was then broken without a quarrel.[3]

By this time, Beerbohm had fallen in love with another of his brother's actresses, Constance Collier. The association was favored by holidays in Dieppe in 1902 and 1903. Constance, however, pleased the Beerbohm family no better than Kilseen had. And Constance found Beerbohm too tepid a lover. On tour she fell in love with her leading man, and in 1904 she wrote to Beerbohm, breaking off the engagement. Beerbohm was saddened by her decision, but he in no way blamed her. In the summer of 1904 he wrote to Turner that, though he would be passing through Dieppe on holiday, he would not stop there. Dieppe was then too intimately associated with Constance.[4]

II *Florence Kahn*

It was after acquaintance with the girlish Cissie Loftus, the companionable Kilseen, and the rather flamboyant Constance Collier that Beerbohm met in 1904 the American actress Florence Kahn, whom he eventually married in 1910. Florence, who had attended a dramatic school in New York, had attracted some favorable attention in the minor part of Chorus in Richard Mansfield's *Henry V*.[5] For a season she was leading lady for James K. Hackett, a less distinguished actor, and she had appeared in two Ibsen plays before arriving in London. An acquaintance had written about her to Beerbohm, since as dramatic critic he might help her to meet the people she needed to know. Beerbohm called, and was at once attracted by her sensitive, reserved manner. In the next six months they spent much time together, and they wrote each other frequently. From the letters that have been published, it appears that the Beerbohm family liked Florence better than either Kilseen or Constance, though she seemed shy and humorless. Max's letters show a very protective attitude toward his "very dear little friend."

From 1904 until 1910 Florence sought engagements with only moderate success[6] in London and New York. In 1908, when she played Rebecca in Ibsen's *Rosmersholm,* Max reviewed the performance with high praise:

> It is difficult to write about Florence Kahn's impersonation of Rebecca; for it is never easy to analyze the merits of great acting. . . . Rebecca is essentially a vessel for implicit, rather than a vehicle for explicit, emotion. . . . In the rare moments when Rebecca breaks through her reserve, Miss Kahn betrays the fact that she has a voice of great power and resonance, and a face that will eloquently express the soul. . . . In its appeal to the emotions, Miss Kahn's acting is not more remarkable than in its appeal to the sense of beauty. Throughout the play, not a tone is inharmonious, not a movement without grace.

Rothenstein, a well-qualified but less partial witness, was almost as enthusiastic about her performance.[7]

In November, 1908, a letter from Beerbohm to Florence proposed marriage. To marry was not a simple decision for either of them. Florence had reason to fear that she could not count heavily on a future in the theater; she was genuinely fond of Max, but she was apprehensive about his clever friends. Max was weary of the social rounds of his London life, and of his weekly stint for *The Saturday Review;* yet he had no assured income from free-lance writing and from his caricatures. In 1906 a visit to Italy had greatly impressed him with the cheapness of living there, and he thought that Florence and he might manage on a small income. She was willing to try, provided that she was sure of Max's affection.

Florence returned to America for a few months, but in July, 1909, she arrived in London. She spent much time with Max's mother and sisters at Upper Berkeley Street, where they now lived, and she frequently entertained Max at her lodgings in Hampstead, near the great Heath. In August, Max went alone to Dieppe, where Turner and other friends were taking their holidays as usual, but for Max, Dieppe was less attractive than formerly. In the autumn he continued as dramatic critic for *The Saturday Review,* but with the understanding that he would resign in the spring. On May 4, 1910, Max and Florence were married at the Paddington registry office. They spent a brief honeymoon in a seaside cottage loaned them by a friend. In July they were in Italy, where they soon found the little house at Rapallo which was to be their permanent home.[8]

III *Periodical Writings: 1895–1898*

The fifteen years during which these restrained romances occurred are not greatly illuminated by them. It is as if one man had done the writing and another had known the ladies. The attraction to Kilseen, for instance, tells us little about the problem Beerbohm faced when he returned to London in the spring of 1895. He, like many others, was well known as an associate of Wilde. When Wilde fell, the courses of many men had to be charted afresh. Although Beerbohm says nothing of this situation in his published letters, one fact is significant: in the Bibliography appended to his *Works* (1896), there is no reference to the article on Wilde in the *Anglo-American Times* of 1893.

Meanwhile, Beerbohm's only publications for the year 1895 are the January *Yellow Book* essay, "1880," written and placed before he went to America; six pieces on dandies, expanded from Oxford material; and two short items in *Sketch*.[9] For a young man who had made such a promising start in 1894, this is a poor showing. It is reasonable to infer that, had the Wilde scandal not occurred, the record might have been otherwise.

In contrast, the next two years show a total of fifty-four publications in newspapers and magazines (twenty, 1896; thirty-four, 1897). Of the 1896 pieces, four were collected in *Works*, published in June, and four others in *More* (1899); of the seven parodies in *The Saturday Review*, the one on George Meredith was revised and included in *A Christmas Garland* (1912). The uncollected pieces range from trivial to important: "Our Lady of Par[agraph]s," is merely an unsigned ironic comment in *The Saturday Review* on the strange way in which Marie Corelli (Mary Mackay, a popular novelist) insisted on the privacy of her personal life but was constantly the subject of press paragraphs giving her views and daily activities; and "Mrs. Meynell's Cowslip Wine" is a polite but firm rejection of Alice Meynell's current book of essays, *Colours of Life*. Besides articles in *The Yellow Book, The Savoy* and *The Saturday Review*, Beerbohm contributed in 1896 to the Chicago *Chap-Book* and to the *Daily Chronicle, Daily Mail, Pageant, Parade* (two annuals), and *To-Morrow*. It is evident that Beerbohm was studying possible markets and trying them out. In 1897, though he published nearly twice as many articles, most of them appeared in the *Daily Mail, To-Morrow*, and *The Saturday Review*.[10]

Analysis of *The Saturday Review* contributions is of particular interest, since it helps to explain his appointment in 1898 as dramatic critic for that journal. When Beerbohm began to contribute to *The Saturday Review* in 1896, it was a weekly of thirty-two double-columned pages. It carried a subhead specifying "politics, literature, and art" as topics to be reviewed. George Bernard Shaw wrote a column on the theater, and there were staff writers for music and art. Several pages were devoted to reviews of new books and a page or so to correspondence. The tone was fresh and intelligent, but paragraphs running a thousand words or more warned off the frivolous reader. The editor was Frank Harris, who had purchased the paper in 1894 and immediately set out to make it the leading weekly in London. Harris, a flamboyant figure, had returned to England after an adventurous youth in which he was for a time an American cowboy; in England, he managed to meet everyone of consequence, married a rich wife, and owned or edited a series of influential magazines. Harris knew Wilde and Shaw, and he was almost as famous a talker as they. Probably through Wilde in 1894, Harris met Beerbohm, liked him, and encouraged him to write for the *Review.*

Beerbohm's first known contribution to *The Saturday Review* (September 12, 1896) was an unsigned review of a book of sentimental verse by Clement Scott, dramatic critic for the *Daily Telegraph.* Scott's volume celebrated holiday joys in this fashion: "Bexhill-on-Sea is the haven for me / Whene'er my nerves are depressed. . . ." As Shelley is the poet of the clouds and Swinburne the poet of the sea, said Max, Mr. Clement Scott is "the poet of the Seaside." To Beerbohm, it was a pity that a man with such a sensitive soul should be forced by circumstances to live in London, frequenting the glaring theater. The authorship of the review was no secret, but Scott treated its anonymity as cowardice. His furious reply in *The Era* was entitled "Come out of Your Hole, Rat." Meanwhile, Reggie Turner had obligingly sent in a letter to the *Saturday,* signed "Lover of Fair Play."[11] On October 10, Max replied with a letter to the *Saturday* captioned "Hold Furious Scot!" "Here am I," he said, "a real, live Rat; young, it may be, but quite calm; rejoicing in a Christian name and surname (both printed below), and in a fairly keen sense of humor." A year later, the feud was renewed when Beerbohm reviewed a volume of Scott's essays on seaside resorts, one of which saluted Brighton as "the unacknowledged Queen of Sussex." The controversy with Scott was trivial enough, but it helped to make the name Max Beerbohm known to readers of *The Saturday Review.*

Meanwhile, Beerbohm had embroiled himself in lesser fashion with one of the most popular authors of the day, Conan Doyle, the creator of Sherlock Holmes. Reviewing Doyle's *Rodney Stone,* a novel about the early nineteenth century, Beerbohm complimented the author on being "the first to have carried the bedside manner into literature"; but he dissented from Doyle's presentation of various dandies of the Regency period. Doyle replied by letter in the next issue, with more wit than malice; below his letter, Beerbohm made some concessions; and the following issue published another letter from Doyle. Thus, through a single brief review, Beerbohm's name was associated with Doyle's in three successive issues. In July, 1897, Beerbohm reviewed Doyle's *Uncle Bernac* in patronizing fashion, with a reminder of the exchange of letters regarding *Rodney Stone.*

In the same month as the first Doyle review (December, 1896), the Christmas Supplement of *The Saturday Review* printed seven short parodies by Beerbohm. Marie Corelli, the sentimental novelist, is made to describe her character thus: "A woman was hastening through the frozen streets of London on the Eve of Christmas last. Over her head and all around her slender frame was stretched a threadbare shawl, tattered in places and with edges sadly frayed." Richard Le Gallienne, a minor poet and whimsical essayist, presents his hero: "It was the Yule Day Eve and the Poet was doing his hair. All the guests in the great, strange house where he was staying, had gone to their white beds, aweary of their revels, save some sterner males who were keeping the holy vigil of Nicotine." The forthright H. G. Wells begins his story with knock-down realism: "Have some more of that stuff? asked Simpson, hoisting his clubfoot onto a vacant chair, and passing his long, bony fingers down the scar that runs vertically from his forehead to his chin. 'I don't mind if I do,' I answered, and he gave me another help." In a self-parody, Max has a dream in which he sees himself strutting, "a creature of high and insolent carriage, bearing beneath my arm a scarlet book, labeled 'The Works of Max Beerbohm.' " The *Works,* his first collection of essays which had been published the previous June, did, indeed, have a scarlet cover.[12]

In *The Saturday Review* of June 12, 1897, Beerbohm published "Words of Consolation and Caution to Mr. Jerome K. Jerome," in which he objected to Jerome's "narrowness of outlook," the "vulgarity and fatuousness of his jokes," and his bad grammar.[13] Jerome was a very popular humorist, but the article drew praise from Robert Buchanan, a well-known critic. In the next issue Buchanan's letter spoke of "how much I love Max and how hugely I enjoy his cheeky comments on the men and manners of the day." Though Beerbohm praised a new edition of Whistler's *The Gentle Art of Making Enemies* (November

27), Whistler took exception to some remarks and wrote an eighteen-line letter to the *Review*, calling Max impertinent and ridiculing his errors in French idiom. Once more Max got the attention he needed to establish himself as a writer.

Besides *The Saturday Review* articles, Beerbohm's most important publications in 1897 were seventeen essays in *The Daily Mail*, which continued from December 5, 1896, to April 17, 1897. Alfred Harmsworth (later Lord Northcliffe) had established the paper in May, 1896, and eagerly sought new talent. Beerbohm's efforts were appreciated, for in August, 1897, he was writing Turner how pleasant he had found the Harmsworths during a weekend visit. The series, entitled "A Commentary by Max Beerbohm," carried this pseudo-serious editorial note: "Our readers will understand that we do not accept the very wide responsibility of identifying ourselves with Mr. Beerbohm's opinions." The opinions expressed in the five essays reprinted in *More* (1899) are harmless enough, though their literary quality justifies preserving them. One is the autobiographical "Going Back to School," quoted in the first chapter of this book. Two others were combined into a single essay on "A. B.," Alfred Bryan, a popular caricaturist whom Beerbohm greatly admired. "Sea-side in Winter" expresses the unconventional but safe opinion that the seaside is more enjoyable in winter than in summer. "An Infamous Brigade" is an attack on firefighters for spoiling the fun of those who gather to watch a lively fire.

The first of the dozen uncollected essays, "The Best Club in Kensington," ridiculed a local debating society, provoked an angry letter denouncing Beerbohm as "a masquerading German," and of course gave Beerbohm a chance to reply in his second article. Was the letter, Max asked, drafted in full Cabinet Council? A serious essay answers Admiral Field's protest against a play representing Lord Nelson's love affair with Lady Hamilton. The scandal, Beerbohm remarks, is now taken as a matter of course, as Parnell's will be in time. Never was there more affection for Nelson than now, and the play does nothing to diminish it. In "The Boat Race," Beerbohm regards the attention given to the annual race between Oxford and Cambridge as excessive. Rowing is really pointless, and the race might well be abandoned; or, he adds with Oxonian condescension, Cambridge might be allowed to win. "Envoi," the last essay of the series, ends with a flourish: "I drop, at length, upon the firm ground of literature. So, with a final snap of my fingers, I wave you farewell, my reader." There is little doubt that Beerbohm could have found a lucrative staff position with *The Daily Mail,* had he desired it. Though he found newspaper writing uncongenial, even as a columnist, the seventeen articles in the *Mail* must have helped to make his name widely known.

On May 28, 1898, Beerbohm published his first article as dramatic critic for *The Saturday Review,* and for the remainder of the year reviews of new plays were his principal work. Before assuming this post, however, he had published in the *Review* five articles later collected in *More* (1899) and *Yet Again* (1909). Of these the most important is "Groups of Myrmidons," one of the best insights into Beerbohm's Oxford experience. Three dramatic criticisms in April and early May are considered in the next chapter. There were a few articles in other magazines, notably a review of Beardsley's *Fifty Drawings* (in the May *Idler*).[14] By May, however, Beerbohm had been so frequent a contributor to *The Saturday Review* that his transition to staff writer was easy and natural, both for himself and his readers.

IV Works *(1896)*

In June, 1896, appeared a slender red-covered volume of wide-margined pages puckishly entitled *The Works of Max Beerbohm with a Bibliography.* The mock-scholarly tone of the title is ingeniously extended by occasional footnotes; generous quotations from "authorities," real or invented; a sprinkling of Greek and French phrases; and numerous references to "my studies." Though Beerbohm had by this time published only sixteen articles (including a letter to the editor), the Bibliography listed in addition some forty caricatures, two published interviews with Beerbohm, and reference to portraits of him by William Rothenstein and Walter Sickert, and to a drawing in *Sketch.* Under *Personalia* are given the date of his birth (authenticated by quotation from the London *Times*), his residence at Oxford, and his London address. Seldom has a first book trumpeted its author so loudly. Though it is stated that the Bibliography was compiled by John Lane, the publisher, it could hardly have been done without Beerbohm's active assistance. The exact circumstances that led to the publication of *Works* are not known; perhaps it was one of Lane's efforts to prop the sagging fortunes of *The Yellow Book,* which ceased publication the following April.

"Dandies and Dandies," the first essay, announces the theme of the volume: Beerbohm does not so much condemn earnest Victorianism; he ignores it and emphasizes pleasure as a main concern of life. How strange, he says, that *Sartor Resartus,* the philosophy of clothes, should have been written by Carlyle, who dressed so badly. Dress is an art too little valued for the simple reason that what is a daily routine is for most people dull. As a dandy, Beerbohm thinks Beau Brummell is the superior of Count D'Orsay because he was more single-minded in his dandyism. Moreover, Brummell is the inventor of nineteenth-century male costume, "so quiet, so reasonable and, I say, emphatically, so beautiful; free from folly or affectation, yet susceptible to quiet ordering; plastic, austere, economical." Clothing can epitomize the individual: "The silk of Mr. Whistler is a real *nocturne,* his linen a symphony *en blanc majeur.*" Beerbohm reserves his highest praise for a Mr. Le V., who for fifty years has kept scrupulous records of his daily dress. In a parody of sentiment Beerbohm ruminates: "Yes, fifty springs have filled his buttonholes with their violets; the snow of fifty winters has been less white than his linen; his boots have outshone fifty sequences of summer suns, and the colors of all those autumns have faded in the dry light of his apparel."[15]

The essay on dandyism is compounded from the *Spirit Lamp* essay of 1893 and from six other essays of 1895 and 1896.[16] In its final form, it is an extension of the first *Yellow Book* essay, "A Defence of Cosmetics," which is revised and retitled in *Works* as "A Pervasion of Rouge." Closely allied to these are two others in the volume, both reprinted from *The Yellow Book.* "King George the Fourth" presents the monarch as "the great voluptuary," but as one who gave as well as received pleasure; "1880" is a remarkable evocation of the year in which Beerbohm was only eight, described as if by a contemporary witness of the fall of Disraeli, of Oscar Wilde's early vogue, and of the fame of Whistler. But, he concludes, "To give an accurate and exhaustive account of that period would need a far less brilliant pen than mine." He looks to such scientific historians as Professor Gardner and the Bishop of Oxford.

"A Good Prince" was a title to attract attention in 1896, for Edward, Prince of Wales, led a gay life that supplied a stream of anecdotes and rumors. Beerbohm's description of the prince in the Green Park, the reference to his "almost blameless life," the fact that "he has never touched a card, never entered a playhouse," rouse the incredulity of the unwary reader. The joke is sustained for a scant three pages and is then quietly exploded: "He stands alone among European princes—but, as yet, only with the aid of a chair." The prince Beerbohm described is now the Duke of Windsor.

"Poor Romeo!" is as close to antiquarianism as Beerbohm ever got. In Bath, the story of Coates is traditional. He was fond of reciting Shakespeare and did it so creditably that a friend offered him the opportunity to appear on the stage as Romeo. So ludicrous was Coates that he was hooted and pelted. Two contemporary accounts, however, ascribe the disorder to a hostile group rather than to the ineptness of Coates. Beerbohm provides a solution in the form of an imagined encounter related as fact. Seeing a print in a Bath shop window, he goes in to purchase it. The shopkeeper's father, it turns out, had known Coates and had seen him return from the theater in good spirits after his performance as Romeo. On receiving a letter the next morning, however, Coates was reduced to tears and left town immediately. The letter he tore into scraps, which the shopkeeper's father had preserved but could never fit together.

Beerbohm says he bought the scraps, and with two days' labor reconstructed the letter. It was from E. T. L. (Emma Tylney Long), a young lady whom Coates's unsuccessful suit had long embarrassed. She had planned the fiasco of the night before and told him in the letter that it was an act of revenge. Coates's later biographer was her agent. Beerbohm concludes the story by reporting the unhappy marriage of Emma, the happy marriage of Coates, and his persistent appearances on the stage, "a salient, pathetic figure." The essay is one of Beerbohm's best blends of comment and narrative, sympathy and amusement. He does not set out to make anyone look ridiculous, as in a parody; but Coates, Emma, and Coates's biographer all appear so. Even the accommodating shopkeeper, treasuring for years scraps of paper he cannot understand, typifies the vanity of antiquarianism. In terms of these people, human nature is indeed too strange to be judged harshly.

"Diminuendo," the seventh and last essay of this first volume, is a slight fabric of reminiscence and speculation. The reminiscence is of Oxford and of Beerbohm's youthful reverence for Walter Pater. Oxford did not satisfy Beerbohm's sense of mystery, nor, at the end of the first term, did London's activity seem attractive. He formed an ambition to live quietly, read the writings of great men, and contemplate the world. Having taken modest lodgings in London, he intends to live the life of an intellectual recluse: "I shall write no more. Already I feel myself to be a trifle outmoded. I belong to the Beardsley period. Younger men, with months of activity before them, with fresher schemes and notions, with newer enthusiasm, have pressed forward since then." But he dates the essay Chicago, 1895! When the essay first appeared in an 1896 annual called *The Pageant*, Beerbohm was already embarked on a vigorous campaign to establish himself in London magazines. The reader who encountered "Diminuendo" in *Works* turned the last page to confront the overblown Bibliography, one hardly consistent with the life of a recluse. "Diminuendo" is, of course, only half serious: Beerbohm does not expect the reader to believe that the brilliant young man about town has retired. Yet, if the essay is half serious, it is half true. Even before the fall of Wilde, Beerbohm must have felt that the mood of *The Yellow Book* was temporary and offered no firm future. The life of the recluse, not literally followed even at Rapallo, did suggest something of the pattern of his life: he would live in the world without losing himself in it. Thus he achieved the mood of detachment, so baffling to reformers and activists, so necessary to the insights he was to offer for the next sixty years in essays, fiction, and caricature that seemed always individual, always Max.

Works is Oscar Wilde estheticism, eighteenth-century sentiment, and uncloyed reminiscence, all made compatible by Beerbohm's wit. Like a good journalist, he does not pretend to tell "all," but only that which will interest. Unlike many journalists, he relies on taste and discrimination rather than on shock. Detachment, not involvement, sets the tone.

V More *(1899)*

Beerbohm's second collection of essays took its title from the stated intention in "Diminuendo" to write "no more." In 1899 Beerbohm had been for a year dramatic critic for *The Saturday Review.* At twenty-seven, he was well established as critic and essayist. *More* includes twenty essays, though the volume is little larger than *Works*, which contained only seven. Six of the essays were reprinted from issues of *The Saturday Review* before he joined its staff; six were drawn from the 1897 series in *The Daily Mail.*

Most of the essays are close to the ephemeral journalism in which the writer takes the easy road to interest by expressing a taste for something unpopular or a distaste for something popular. The subjects themselves are often shallow, but the essays are usually interesting for turns of phrase and for some individuality in point of view. The amalgam of rebellion and conservatism was beginning to form; he rejected convention when it was stupid and valued tradition when it was interesting. Among his tastes are fires (for their beauty); the seaside, when deserted in the off-season; sign boards (instead of the crowded display windows); old-time music halls (for their vulgarity); Ouida, the popular novelist (for her vitality in lieu of "art"). Among Beerbohm's distastes are Madame Tussaud's waxworks (ingenious but abortive and depressing), the crowded Strand (so full of pretense), serious music (though for other reasons Covent Garden is amusing), *Punch* (its quality has declined), sculpture (a lost art), overzealous planning to "beautify" London, the overaffectionate attitude toward children, bicycles (especially for women), knighthood (it is too common now), and even royalty itself (an absurd institution).

From this volume a recent selection of the best of Beerbohm[17] reprints only three essays: "Some Words on Royalty," "A Cloud of Pinafores," and "Groups of Myrmidons." The first two of these are characteristic enough, but they might well be passed over for "On Going Back to School." This essay and "Groups of Myrmidons" are not only the best autobiographical comments we have on Beerbohm's Charterhouse and Oxford experience; they are witty glimpses of growing up, free of the sentimentality and false rage that often vitiate such accounts.

Yet, when we contemplate abandoning the other essays, we recall many passages too good to lose, all of them better in context than in isolated quotation. The English public is admonished: "Only remember this, you are very dull dogs, who do not deserve comic papers half so good as *Punch* and the *Times.*" In the essay on actors Beerbohm remarks: "Theatrical reminiscence is the most awful weapon in the armory of old age." After the description of the waxworks in Madame Tussaud's museum, "that morgue of upstanding corpses," how effective is the simple, commonplace concluding sentence: "Ah! it was good to be in the street!" Justifying his delight in fires, Beerbohm brilliantly turns conventional logic inside out when he says: "The sentimentalist may prattle of life-saving, but we must think, rather, of the greatest happiness of the greatest number." It is memorable, too, when Beerbohm, whose natural preference is for "delicate and elaborate ingenuities of form," praises Ouida as an illustration of the truth that "writers of enormous vitality never are artistic."[18]

More neither surprised nor disappointed readers who remembered *Works.* The second volume, against the background of weekly dramatic criticism in *The Saturday Review*, was the product of an established writer, still only twenty-seven.

VI *Activities, 1896–1900*

In 1896 Beerbohm sent a copy of *Works* to Edmund Gosse, then in his mid-forties and a very influential man in literary London. In acknowledgment, Gosse sent an invitation to one of his famous "at-homes," informal receptions on Sunday afternoons. Beerbohm became a frequent visitor, and he was often invited to stay for supper and for the flow of more intimate talk that followed. Gosse was privately educated and had served for eight years as assistant librarian of the British Museum. He became translator for the Board of Trade, held a lectureship at Cambridge from 1884 to 1890, and in 1904 became librarian to the House of Lords, a post of social as well as literary distinction. Gosse wrote biographical and critical essays, especially about seventeenth-century writers. He early became familiar with Scandinavian literature and helped to introduce Ibsen to the English public.

In literary London, Gosse knew nearly everyone who mattered, and he was very helpful to young writers. Through Gosse, Beerbohm met Henry James, Whistler, and many others. In an uncollected essay on Andrew Lang,[19] then a prolific writer, Beerbohm has left an amusing account of how Gosse would bring together guests that he thought might find one other interesting. Beerbohm, who disliked Scots on principle, found Lang thorny and uncommunicative. Years later it was to Gosse that Beerbohm dedicated his last major book of drawings (*Observations*, 1925).

In December, 1896, *Works* was followed by Beerbohm's first collection of drawings, *Caricatures of Twenty-five Gentlemen* (discussed in the chapter on caricature). A contemporary described, no doubt with some exaggeration, the effect of this volume: "Twenty-five bombs dropped in Piccadilly from twenty-five Zeppelins would not have created a greater sensation. As I write, the remarks come back to me as to the brutality, the cruelty, and, the artists said, the crudeness of his work."[20] Artistic merit aside, the volume of caricatures, like the numerous magazine and newspaper articles, drew attention to Beerbohm. By the end of 1896 he was a Personality.

VII *Early Fiction*

One result of such popularity was John Lane's publication of a small book, *The Happy Hypocrite*, in April, 1897. This work was Beerbohm's last contribution to *The Yellow Book* (October, 1896). *The Happy Hypocrite* is the story of Lord George Hell, an eighteenth-century rake "rather like Caligula, with a dash of Falstaff." One night at the theater, Lord George falls hopelessly in love with a young actress named Jenny Mere. "My wealth, my rank, my irremediable love for you, I throw them at your feet," he declares, but in vain. Jenny Mere replies that she cannot accept him because his face is not saintly. In despair, Lord George visits a mask maker and adopts a disguise. Jenny Mere is immediately won by the new admirer with the saintly face. The lovers reject the corrupt city and find an idyllic home in a beautiful wood. When a jealous dancer pursues them and unmasks Lord George, his real face has lost its evil lines and has become saintly under the mask. Jenny Mere brushes aside the deception and accepts him as he is: "They were alone in the garden now. Nor lay the mask any longer upon the lawn, for the sun had melted it."[21]

The Happy Hypocrite is a curious period piece. In part it is a fairy tale in the manner of Oscar Wilde, who, without a sense of incongruity, could turn from sophisticated cynicism to the simply sentimental. In part the story is a parody of Wilde's *The Picture of Dorian Gray,* a sensational novel of 1891, in which the portrait of Dorian as a handsome young man gradually reflects the evil of Dorian's life. In part, also, *The Happy Hypocrite* is, like the essay on Romeo Coates in *Works,* an evocation of the eighteenth century, decorated with footnotes and identifications of actual places.

Though the story is unlikely to win readers for Beerbohm today,[22] it had a fascination for his contemporaries. In 1900 Beerbohm dramatized it successfully as a one-act curtain raiser. In *A Variety of Things* (1928) he reprinted the story, and, perhaps as a result, it was then expanded by Clemence Dane to a three-act play, with moderate success. In advice to the actors presenting the play in 1900, Beerbohm said that all the characters should be made up and played as caricatures, but for him caricature always had an element of truth.[23] Many years later, S. N. Behrman discussed the story with Beerbohm. It would be easy, Behrman said, if one could achieve beauty or goodness by simply buying a mask. Beerbohm replied: "But oh, you have to live *up* to the mask, you know. . . . Lord George lived *up* to the mask. His love for Jenny made it possible for him to do it" (p. 299). But in the story, Lord George's reform remains a fantasy. For Beerbohm, the story was linked with Cissy Loftus, whom he had often referred to as Jenny Mere.

Two other early stories, reprinted in *A Variety of Things,* were first published in gift books of 1897. "The Story of the Small Boy and the Barley-Sugar" is about childhood disillusionment. Tommy spends an unexpected penny on barley sugar, which the fairy-shopgirl tells him will make his wish come true with every bite. Sharing the sweet with a little girl named Jill, Tommy explains its wonderful power. She seizes it and stuffs the whole of it in her mouth. When Tommy protests and reminds her that she did not even stop to make a wish, she replies: "Oh, yes, I did. . . . I wished you hadn't eaten that first bit." The other story, "Yai and the Moon," is an Oriental tale in the then popular sentimental vein. A widower's little daughter rejects the marriage arranged for her. Going out to sea in a boat, she tells the Moon of her sadness. The next morning the Sun discovers her body floating on the water. "After all," he concludes, "it does not do for these human beings to have ideas above their station."

These early stories remind us that even in the essays Beerbohm was fond of narrative. In "Poor Romeo" there is genuine suspense as Beerbohm presents factually his theory of what really happened that night in the Bath theater. Probably as early as 1898 he began to develop the idea for the Oxford novel, *Zuleika Dobson,* and in the three stories just summarized there are some anticipations of it. Lord George Hell, like the young Duke in the novel, is the victim of love at first sight; and, like the Duke, he is at first spurned. The little girl who ate the barley sugar, like Zuleika, is a realist not fully understood by her lover. The girl in "Yai and the Moon" represents youthful sorrow. Though these early stories are minor achievements, they throw light on Beerbohm's development from essayist to novelist.

VIII *Periodical Writings: 1899–1910*

Besides the 453 dramatic criticisms for *The Saturday Review* during his twelve years as staff writer, Beerbohm published some sixty other articles, a few of them in the *Review* itself, but most of them in a dozen other journals. Of these, perhaps the most important were the ten articles on Italy published as a series in *The Daily Mail* in 1906. It was his first appearance in that paper since the seventeen articles published in 1896–97 at the invitation of the owner, Alfred Harmsworth. It was Harmsworth who proposed that Beerbohm go to Italy and write about his impressions. The trip of about five weeks in the early autmn of 1906 included visits to Venice, Padua, Verona, and Florence; it was wholly enjoyable. The following year, Beerbohm spent a holiday with friends at Portofino, near Rapallo; and gradually the idea of living in Italy coalesced with his romantic interest in Florence Kahn.[24]

The ten *Daily Mail* articles appeared in November and December. The first described lugubriously the rail trip through the Swiss mountains: "I had never wished to see them, but they glowered so intently at me while I breakfasted that I had to return the stare. . . . Up, up, and down, down, bulge infinitely, unmeaningly, these clumsy precipices; and on them crawl certain parasites—a nation by courtesy." The next four essays describe his wanderings in Venice, "a plexus of mystic alleys." He read Ruskin's famous description of Saint Mark's, admired it, looked at Saint Mark's itself, and decided that even Ruskin was inadequate; but he said, "I would give almost anything to have written that passage." He commented on the depredations of "that brute Napoleon" and approved the restoration to Saint Mark's of the four great bronze horses after their sojourn in Paris. Thinking of James's *The Aspern Papers,* he speculated that "it must have been there, in *that* palace" that the Misses Bordereau lived. He found no evidence that Venice had deteriorated, as seasoned travelers had reported; Venice absorbed change. The sixth essay, captioned "He goes to Padua, but—," told with fictional suspense how he drastically shortened his stay in Padua, for he was irresistibly compelled by the charms of Venice to return there. The seventh essay dealt with Verona, the next two with Florence. Observing American tourists in the Uffizi Gallery, he commented: "They do not even pretend to enjoy it. They perform it grimly, as a duty they will later look back upon with satisfaction—self-satisfaction." The last article concluded: "When I die, Venice will be found graven on my heart."

Late in life Beerbohm told his friend S. N. Behrman that the *Daily Mail* essays were "no good" (18). It is hard to see why he thought so, and fortunate that he at least combined parts of them into "A Stranger in Venice," one of the most charming essays in *A Variety of Things* (1928). By omitting comments on the Swiss and on the trips to Verona and Florence, Beerbohm achieves greater unity. The hurried return from Padua is used in narrative fashion as a concluding gesture of love for Venice. The original articles, however, give a fuller account of an important episode in Beerbohm's life; and they are still worth reading as journalism touched with genius.

Other important essays of this period are his estimates of Beardsley and Wilde. Beerbohm wrote two articles on Beardsley: the first, a laudatory review of *Fifty Drawings* (1897); the second, a tribute published in 1898 shortly after Beardsley's death. The review, never republished, is valuable as a brief technical study. The second, included in *A Variety of Things,* is a defense of the artist on broader grounds. Beerbohm emphasizes the ceaseless activity of a man who knew he would die young, and the precociousness of Beardsley's talent. Beerbohm concedes that some of the drawings were morbid and that they might be sincerely rejected by some tastes. Yet morbidity, he points out, is characteristic of youth. Over against the morbidity is set the gaiety and kindness of Beardsley's life at home and with his friends, and his refusal to be discouraged by criticism. Beerbohm tells with special pleasure the story of how Beardsley published under other names some conventional drawings; reviewers then urged Beardsley to study the technique of these fictitious artists. "No man ever *saw* more than Beardsley," Beerbohm concludes, and that was the basis of his genius.[25]

The tribute to Wilde appended to a dramatic review of 1900 has been mentioned; it was followed in 1905 by a review of *De Profundis,* entitled "Lord of Language." Beerbohm begins by saying that neither Whistler nor Wilde was ever taken seriously as a moralist or as a man of practical wisdom. Wit was the least important of Wilde's gifts; he was primarily a poet. *De Profundis* is "the artistic essay of an artist," playing with ideas, playing with emotions. Wilde's humility is "the luxurious complement of his pride." The phrase "lord of language" comes from a passage in which Wilde referred to the death of his mother. Beerbohm concludes with this final judgment: "Except Ruskin in his prime, no modern writer has achieved through prose the limpid and lyrical effects that were achieved by Oscar Wilde." In this review the only reference to Wilde's downfall is the comment that he was "the spectator of his own tragedy."[26]

Why did Beerbohm never reprint this eloquent tribute to Wilde, and perhaps also the note of 1900? Why did he wait until 1928 to reprint the one essay on Beardsley, and why was the review of *Fifty Drawings* left uncollected? Might not these four essays, with recollections of Rothenstein and others that Beerbohm knew well, have formed the basis of an important book about the 1890's? Friends must have urged such a project upon him. His failure to undertake it was characteristic. As time went on, his feelings became too deeply involved. His association with Wilde and Beardsley was well known. He would not have suppressed his early opinions of them even if he could have done so. But neither would he emphasize those opinions. Rothenstein could reminisce in three volumes if he chose. Beerbohm would be selective in his recollections, and he would subordinate them to other claims on public attention.

IX Yet Again *(1909)*

Beerbohm's third collection of essays was titled, like *More*, as a reminder of the announced decision in *Works* to write "no more." The thirty-one essays included show the level of expert and individual journalism exhibited in *More*, but they hardly go beyond it. The essays were originally magazine contributions, the by-products of years principally devoted to dramatic reviews.

As in *More*, Beerbohm's distastes are prominent; and they are sometimes hackneyed and oversimple. In "General Elections" he professes a lack of interest in politics. The plight of the poor inclines him to socialism; but, when even Arnold's Barbarians (aristocrats) are being overcome, he is content with things as they are; he feels only a sporting interest in the outcome of elections. In "The House of Commons Manner," Beerbohm laments the decline of style; the age of oratory belonged to the age of port, and it is gone. A page of parody shows the mumbling now current: "seems to me to me—to me to *be*." Only parliamentary reporters can construct a cosmos from the chaos of debate. Allied to the low state of debate is "A Pathetic Imposture," an objection to editorial writers who refuse to say simply that Lord Rosebery made a paradox; instead, they provide such standard elegant variations as "Lord Rosebery, with seeming conviction, expressed a sentiment which, we venture to assert, is nearly akin to the paradoxical."[27]

Antiquarianism, like politics, is an easy target. Beerbohm begins his essay "Whistler's Writing" by declaring that he is no bibliophile; he dislikes uncut pages, and he would willingly light his cigarette with the margin of a page of Shakespeare's First Folio. "Morris for May-Day" points to the folly of artificially reviving such relics as the Morris dance. "A Ragged Regiment" describes the dreariness of effigies found in such places as Westminster Abbey. Thackeray, he remarks, would have responded differently: "Dear gentleman, how promptly and copiously he would have wept and moralized here, in his grandest manner, with that perfect technical mastery which makes even the tritest and shallowest sermons sound remarkable, his hollowest sentiment ring true" (244). This single sentence is an example of the casual asides that make even the most trivial of Beerbohm's essays enjoyable and rewarding.

"Shakespeare's Birthday" concludes with encouragement to Baconians. Should they succeed in their efforts, the plays would remain, and a great deal of tiresome hero worship would disappear. "The Decline of the Graces" is a mock-serious praise of *The Young Lady's Book* of 1829. Will no one, Beerbohm asks, revise that "Manual of Elegant Recreations, Exercises, and Pursuits," adapting it to present needs? The reader who turns to the last essay in the volume, a meditation on George Morland's painting "The Visit," finds a directly critical account of old-fashioned manners: the priggishness of the model children, the dullness of the daily routine, the Olympian majesty of Papa in the background, and the exaggerated delight of the visiting lady, who holds a basket of fruit on her lap.

"The Humour of the Public" is a thoughtful examination of stereotyped humor. By "public" Beerbohm explains that he means "that vast number of human animals who are in the lowest grade of intelligence," without reference, he adds, to social classes (252). His conclusions are similarly uncomplimentary: the public, thus defined, responds only to violent and obvious humor. In the comic papers, drawings are often quite skillful; but "Nothing is sadder than to see the hand of an artist wasted by alliance to a vacant mind, a common spirit" (256).

Considerably fresher in approach are some of the essays which develop favorable responses. "Fire" begins by comparing the fire in the grate with a caged lion. The primitive quality of fire is part of its charm, and can best be savored alone, particularly in a guest room after saying goodnight to the host. In contrast to the other elements, "flames aspire, flying back towards the heaven they came from" (7). In "Dulcedo Judiciorum" ("The Charm of Trials"), Beerbohm finds the courtroom superior to the theater in dramatic interest. Famous trials, he suggests, might be reproduced in theaters; admission might even be charged to current trials.

In this volume, the essay on Whistler is the only extended treatment of an individual. First published at the time of Whistler's death in 1903, it is primarily an evaluation of the artist as writer. Whistler's writings, Beerbohm thinks, have been underestimated because as a writer Whistler was an amateur; but the amateur approach gives freshness to his writings. Whistler's paintings express his reverence; his writings express his harshness and vanity. His "insults always stuck—stuck and spread round the insulted, who found themselves at last encased in them, like flies in amber. You may shed a tear over the flies, if you will. I am content to laud the amber" (119).

A few essays follow a narrative pattern very close to fiction. In "A Club in Ruins" Beerbohm begins by describing the ruins of a building formerly used as a clubhouse. A bearded stranger, asking directions to this club, is informed that it no longer exists. Just in from Australia, the stranger is incensed; he has paid his dues regularly for years. " 'And now. . . .' He filled up his aposiopesis with an uncouth gesture, signifying, 'I might as well get back to Australia' " (61). The title word of the essay "Sympat"[28] comes from a friendly Brazilian, met in foreign parts. Their brief association as travelers was pleasant, but later, in London, the Brazilian becomes tedious when he tries to instruct Beerbohm about his own city. "Sympat" thus stands for the agreeable but impermanent attraction known to travelers.

"Midnight Express" is a traveler's fancy about a vaguely forbidding man—possibly a murderer—who occupies the same train compartment. Nothing happens, except that the man tells a reassuring story of his quite ordinary life. "Homecoming" tells of a similar chance meeting in a Dover buffet after a channel crossing. A nattily dressed young man, not at all depressed by a sleepless night, flirts with the barmaid and on the station platform winks at Beerbohm. "Preeminently, he was one of those who have made England what it is. . . . I knew him to be a stranger sight, a more memorable and instructive, than any of the fair sights I had been seeing" (231). Beerbohm then tears up the notes he had gathered for a travel book.

The last nine essays in the volume are grouped as "Words for Pictures." The comment on Corot's "Macbeth and the Witches" illustrates the method. Beerbohm begins with a dramatized description: "Look! Across the plain yonder, those three figures, dark and gaunt against the sky. . . . Who are they? What are they?" The long paragraph fills out with words what an observant viewer would see on the canvas. That Macbeth and Banquo are not distinguishable is not a fault but a beauty.

Corot, because as a Frenchman he had no reverence for Shakespeare's text, has caught the mood of the scene: "for us Corot's brush-work fills the place of Shakespeare's music." Usually Beerbohm describes the chosen picture sympathetically, even sentimentally, in the Pre-Raphaelite manner. Elsewhere Beerbohm vigorously denounces illustrated books on the ground that the illustrator is an interloper. In "Words for Pictures" he does not reflect that verbal interpretation of pictures is just as open to attack. One is as blameworthy—or defensible—as the other. "Words for Pictures" is dated in a way that few of Beerbohm's other writings are.[29]

Yet Again is perhaps the least important of the collections of essays. For his volume of selections, S. C. Roberts included only "Fires" and "Whistler's Writing." The others are readable but, on the whole, trivial. The comments on pictures seem especially "made-up" rather than strongly motivated. The volume indicates what Beerbohm himself knew: he needed relief from the chore of weekly reviewing.

X *Beerbohm in 1910*

When Beerbohm left his staff position on *The Saturday Review* in May, 1910, his future was uncertain; but he could feel some confidence as he looked back on the preceding fifteen years. He had recovered from the fall of Wilde and the demise of *The Yellow Book* and *The Savoy*. His essays had been welcomed by a dozen or more publications besides *The Saturday Review*. He could point to three collections of essays: *Works, More,* and *Yet Again.* He had published three collections of drawings: *Caricatures of Twenty-five Gentlemen, The Poets' Corner,* and *A Book of Caricatures.* There were still many uncollected essays in the magazine files, and leisure would give him opportunity to write more. He had in progress a novel (*Zuleika Dobson*) which he was anxious to finish. If he were ever going to break away from the routine of dramatic reviewer, now was the time. His favorable reputation as reviewer would be remembered and would help the sale of anything he wrote or drew. It was Florence Kahn, of course, who without argument helped him to see his way to take the chance. When we consider what he accomplished in the next fifteen years, it was a lucky chance, for much of Beerbohm's best work was done after 1910.

CHAPTER 3

Dramatic Criticism: 1898-1910

AFTER three lively years as dramatic critic for *The Saturday Review,* George Bernard Shaw published his "Valedictory" on May 21, 1898.[1] The conclusion has been quoted many times, but it remains inevitable in any account of Beerbohm's career: "The younger generation is knocking at the door, and as I open it there steps sprightly in the incomparable Max." This vivid rhetorical flourish is, however, slightly misleading. In less than two years Beerbohm's name had become familiar to readers of the *Review* through some twenty-five contributions, not to mention letters to the editor provoked by them. Even as dramatic critic, Beerbohm was not altogether new. On April 9, under the caption "Gibiesse [G.B.S.] Oblige", Beerbohm had objected vigorously to Shaw's praise of William Heinemann's play, *Summer Moths.* What Shaw is saying, Beerbohm counters, is that a bad play is a good play if it attacks convention. Heinemann, he thinks, is merely an imitator of Ibsen, and not a very good one.

It must have been about this time that Shaw either suggested or approved Beerbohm as his successor. An unpublished letter from Beerbohm to Shaw,[2] dated "April," expresses regret that Shaw is retiring and doubt that Beerbohm himself is qualified to replace him. Following this letter, Beerbohm wrote a two-part attack on Shaw's *Mrs. Warren's Profession,* which appeared May 14 and 21 (the same issue as Shaw's "Valedictory"). In this play, Beerbohm charges, Shaw is motivated by direct moral purpose in exposing hypocritical attitudes toward prostitution. Though the play has force, it lacks convincing characters. To the traditional axiom, "No conflict; no drama," Beerbohm adds "No sympathy; no conflict." In the second article, after expressing sympathy for Shaw's recent illness, Beerbohm asserts that Shaw's view of life, like Plato's philosophy, rests "on a profound ignorance of human nature." When Shaw forgets about moral purpose, he is fantastic and frivolous: "it is then that his plays are good."

Thus, when readers confronted Beerbohm's first official article on May 28, "Why I Ought Not to Have Become a Dramatic Critic,"[3] he might reasonably have expected them not to take it too seriously. It was fun to protest, however. He considered himself a poor substitute for the brilliant Shaw. He took, he said, "neither emotional nor intellectual pleasure" in drama. He had no critical theory nor any knowledge of such traditional critics as Hazlitt, Lamb, and George Henry Lewes. He could, it was true, "recite backwards" most of the successful plays of the past ten years; and he had (through his half-brother Herbert Beerbohm Tree) an acquaintance with many actors. He could only console himself, he concluded, by reflecting that his lot as critic was less uncomfortable than that of a porter in the underground railway.

I *Approach to Drama*

Witty exaggeration aside, it is really true that Beerbohm approached dramatic criticism with no formal theory and, apparently, no intention of forming one. He trusted his own taste, though he was willing to examine it, to revise it, and even to admit errors. He stated his response to a play and tried to explain the reasons for it. If, from time to time, he seemed to commit himself to large abstract principles, he felt free to limit their application in later essays. His writing about the theater thus retained the quality of good talk: omission of the obvious, exaggeration for effect, and willingness to say part of the truth well. In the last article he wrote, Beerbohm confessed: "I do not recall that I have once sat down eager to write, or that I have once written with ease and delight."[4] Such was his art that his readers never suspected the anguish with which he devoted his Thursdays to composing his weekly review.

Beerbohm recognized certain limitations of the theater. It existed for the upper class, and always had, even in Athens and in Elizabethan England. In modern England he thought the public virtually incapable of esthetic pleasure of any kind, and the very hours of performance tended to reduce the theater to mere recreation. He accepted Realism as the major vital impulse of his time, but his conception of it he carefully distinguished from reality itself. Dialogue, for instance, must be edited and compressed; yet in a play by Somerset Maugham (March 5, 1904) he objected to an epigram: "Matrimony, like hanging, is rather a desperate remedy." To Beerbohm, the rhythm of actual speech would be better represented thus: "Matrimony is like hanging. It is rather a desperate remedy." To this illustration, Beerbohm added the comment: "Nothing that does not sound as if it could be spoken by a real person should be put to the lips of a puppet; but, gentle syllogist, not everything that sounds so should be put there."

Realism should not rule out fantasy, since good fantasy has its roots in reality. Melodrama was repeatedly characterized as a dead form because of its stereotyped avoidance of reality, and its failure to project credible characters. A good dramatic idea, Beerbohm thought, was one that enabled the dramatist to show fresh observation of a human situation. "If a man is dull," he said in *Theatres* (46), "rightness in him does not conciliate me."

A constant threat to the sense of reality was the predominance of the upper class in theater audiences. Playwrights were likely to present only aristocratic characters—"these eternal duchesses" (November 21, 1903)—and they were likely to take aristocrats at their own mistaken evaluation of themselves. "Old Heidelberg," with its sentimental emphasis of a prince's sacrifice of true love, seemed false. Beerbohm reminded his readers (March 28, 1903) that there are rewards as well as sacrifices in kingship; he urged his overenthusiastic critical colleagues "to dry their eyes and pull themselves together." Beerbohm welcomed plays that dealt seriously with servants (May 5, 1900), and he even complimented one playwright who had the courage to present sympathetically an old maid (June 13, 1903). Yet in Maxim Gorky's *The Lower Depths* Beerbohm found neither story nor character: "Gorky on the stage is merely a bore, and a disgusting bore" (1903).

Since the life of our own time is not likely to seem beautiful to us, it is natural to look for drama in the life of earlier times. Yet effective illusion is almost impossible to create when historical or literary figures are brought on stage. A play on Cromwell (September 15, 1900) and one on Napoleon (1903) Beerbohm thought failures; indeed, to him, the use of historical figures was likely to encourage lavish spectacles, as in Sardou's *Robespierre* (April 22, 1899). Instead of the mere trestles, planks, and passion required by Dumas, Sardou says in effect: "Give me an exciting period, two hundred supers, and sixty-two acting parts, and Sir Henry Irving shall do the rest."

As for literary figures, the stage rarely gives the illusion that they are writers. Sardou's play on Dante was reviewed under the caption "Antidantedote" (May 9, 1903). Dante's life Beerbohm thought highly undramatic: "no jolly good fellow he, but a harsh, narrow saint." No doubt Dante "was a pure flame and dwelt apart," but Beerbohm did not care to see Sardou "light his gas from it." Similarly, he did not welcome dramatized novels. *Tess of the D'Urbervilles* on stage (1900) is merely melodrama, though in Hardy's novel the action is elevated by the "poetic haze" of his descriptive style.

Beerbohm's criticism of dramatic technique was necessarily brief, for he could not assume that his readers would know the play well enough for him to consider its technique in any detail. He would sometimes say merely that the first act was unnecessary, or that the last act was too long. He was skillful in ridiculing a play by reducing it to its basic stereotyped situations, but he could sometimes turn this method to positive account. St. John Hankin's *The Return of the Prodigal* (1905), he points out, illustrates the second most obvious way of telling the old story. Instead of emphasizing the father, Hankin effectively makes the conflict between the brothers central when the younger one returns from failure in Australia. In doing so, Hankin rejects Shaw's influence and develops a comedy of conflict rather than a preachment. At one point, the prodigal admits that his life has not been admirable; but, he says, "it was devilish interesting." The defect of the play, Beerbohm thinks, is that this "interesting" side of his life is not sufficiently suggested.

Stereotyped characters and situations were frequently criticized. The fashionable young man, so familiar as a supporting character, was probably derived from Thackeray's Marquis of Farintosh, in *The Newcomes*. In E. Temple Thurston's *John Chilcote, M.P.* (1905), the device of two men looking so alike that the wife of one mistakes the other man for him, though possible in a magazine story, cannot create the illusion of reality on the stage. Mr. Israel Zangwill, a dramatist of some talent, has been misled by Jerome K. Jerome into providing such "simple exercises" as having an absent-minded character pour tea on the carpet instead of into his cup (1904). More central stereotypes are the obstacles that stud the path of lovers, and that "dramatic moment when the hero and heroine gasp, blush, gaze into each other's eyes" (September 23, 1905).

More subtle points are Beerbohm's discussion of the importance of surprise, the necessity of a degree of anticlimax at the end of a play, and the usefulness of soliloquies. Though soliloquies have been discarded, largely because of the influence of Ibsen, Beerbohm points to the novel, and says that they are sometimes justified and may be interesting. The confidant, "our old friend," may be a more clumsy device than the soliloquy. Far from claiming omniscience, Beerbohm frankly admits that he cannot prophesy the stageworthiness of a play. Shaw's *Man and Superman* seemed to him, as he read the text, a poor play. When it was successfully produced, he admitted his error.[5]

Thus Beerbohm carried forward what Shaw described as the "siege laid to the theater of the nineteenth century"[6] during his three years as Beerbohm's predecessor on *The Saturday Review*. Beerbohm's admiration for Ibsen was much more moderate than Shaw's; and, though no "bardolator", his approach to Shakespeare was more sympathetic and discriminating.

Beerbohm had no thought of reprinting his dramatic criticisms until a collected edition of his works was begun in 1920. In 1924 *Around Theatres* appeared as the eighth and ninth volumes of that edition. In the Epistle Dedicatory addressed to the stage designer Gordon Craig, Beerbohm is apologetic. The idea of such a collection, he said, was "ghastly." He "shrank from burrowing down among those conscientious old efforts and bringing up some of them to be read in broad daylight." The 153 reviews selected stood the daylight of 1924 very well, and they are still both entertaining and rewarding. The 318 uncollected pieces in the files of *The Saturday Review* are almost, and often quite, as good as those in *Around Theatres*, as is evident from the quotations made from them in this chapter.

II *Shaw*

In 1898, at forty-two, Shaw was still having difficulty in getting his plays produced; for his great popularity did not come until the 1920's. Beerbohm wrote eighteen reviews of Shaw's work, twelve of which he included in *Around Theatres*. The first, of

The Devil's Disciple (1899), is one of the best. Beerbohm congratulates Shaw on having written a superb melodrama (such as Shaw himself would have condemned) and then turning it into farce in the last act. Dick, the scapegrace who offers to sacrifice himself for the revolutionary minister, all because of hopeless love for the minister's wife, is Shaw's "first really human and convincing character." Shaw, no doubt, who "imagines emotion to be an unfortunate and not inevitable nuisance," had other intentions. The review closes with anticipation of Shaw's preface to the published play and with a paragraph of parody as good as Beerbohm's better-known ones. Shaw is made to comment that General Burgoyne is "a realist, whose only illusion is that he is a very agreeable fellow."

In "Mr. Shaw Crescent" (1901), Beerbohm reviewed very favorably Shaw's published *Plays for Puritans*. These plays, Beerbohm thought, showed Shaw's real genius for comedy; they are thus a notable advance from his serious plays, often too obviously indebted to Ibsen. *Caesar and Cleopatra*, which Beerbohm had not seen on the stage, seemed to him as amusing as *The Devil's Disciple*; both plays were extremely readable. *Captain Brassbound's Conversion*, however, was "not masterly." The prefaces, notes, and stage directions of this volume Beerbohm found perhaps "even more interesting than the plays themselves." Moreover, there is evidence that Shaw (now forty-five) has been reading Plato, "a very proper habit in a young writer." The republication of an early novel, *Cashel Byron's Profession* (1882), gave Beerbohm opportunity to comment on the essential nature of Shaw's genius (1901). The novel "tallies with all his recent work," but his attempt to persuade his readers that his pugilist has a contempt for his profession goes further than the truth. Shaw fails as a creator of character, yet is himself immortal as a personality.

The revival of *Mrs. Warren's Profession* (1902) gave Beerbohm occasion to reiterate his 1898 criticism of the play. It is "a powerful and stimulating, even an ennobling piece of work," but it is a failure as a tragic play because Mrs. Warren, the madame of a house of prostitution, and her daughter, who during the play learns of her mother's occupation, are not convincing characters. The following year (1903) Beerbohm refused to consider the published *Man and Superman* as a play; the discussion is captioned "Mr. Shaw's New Dialogues." To Beerbohm, the characters, a prig and a minx, discuss their ideas in a manner strongly reminiscent of Plato; the writing is brilliant but wrongheaded. In an aside (*Theatres*, 472), Beerbohm referred to this judgment as a "howler," since the play proved delightful when staged. In *John Bull's Other Island* (1904) Beerbohm considers Broadbent, the Englishman who runs for an Irish parliamentary seat, to be one of Shaw's best characters. The play is "a masterpiece of observation and satire," but critics object because it does not have the usual neat love story.

After a command performance of *Major Barbara* made Shaw famous overnight, Beerbohm was amused at the dilemma of his fellow critics as they confronted the new production (1905). Those who resented Shaw because he was unpopular are now forced to accept him. Those who praised Shaw because he was unpopular are now dismayed by his popularity. Beerbohm himself thinks that Major Barbara, the Salvation Army daughter, and her industrialist father show real imagination, even though the play has little action in the conventional sense. Shaw's "technique is peculiar because his purpose is peculiar. But it is not the less technique."

Doctor's Dilemma (1906), reviewed under the caption "Mr. Shaw's Roderick Hudson," is shown to be analogous to Henry James's early novel about a young artist without a moral sense. After raising various objections, Beerbohm breaks off: "Why have I been carping all this while about the central figure, instead of expressing the joy that the whole brilliant play gave me, and trying to communicate something of that joy to you? I evidently haven't learnt my business." *The Philanderer* (1907) Beerbohm found somewhat dated in its presentation of the New Woman. The play is too high-spirited to be serious, too serious to be high-spirited. Charteris, the philanderer, is too unpleasant to be accepted in the context given him. *Arms and the Man* Beerbohm did not see in its first production in 1894, but when the play was revived (1908), he found it "a brilliant thing." The plot about the realistic soldier who exposes the heroine's romantic illusions he thought overingenious. In comparison with Shaw's later plays, however, *Arms and the Man* is "shrill in tone, and narrow in outlook, and shallow." *Getting Married* (1908) and *Misalliance* (1910) were unsatisfactory to Beerbohm.

Both plays treat marriage with a mixture of incongruous elements, and the young people in them are unconvincing.

The six uncollected reviews of Shaw do not greatly change the plus and minus verdicts in *Around Theatres,* yet they are well worth reading. The "unofficial" review of *Mrs. Warren's Profession* on May 14 and 21, 1898, was probably omitted from the collection for the simple reason that a review of the 1902 revival was included. *Captain Brassbound's Conversion* Beerbohm found poorly fused and vitiated by Shaw's idealistic appeals to reason (December 29, 1900). On the other hand, he thought *The Admirable Bashville,* Shaw's blank-verse adaptation of his novel about the noble-minded pugilist (*Cashel Byron's Profession),* even better on the stage than when he read the text (June 13, 1903). Noting a German production of *Man and Superman* (June 8, 1907), Beerbohm begins by saying "We do not deserve Mr. Shaw." Having read the play many times, Beerbohm concludes: "In no other work of his is one so struck by the force and agility of his brain, by the spontaneity of his humor, and by the certainty of his wit." Of an American edition of Shaw's dramatic reviews, Beerbohm wrote (April 27, 1907) that they constituted a permanent book. Shaw, he thought, made every word tell, though he cared nothing for beauty and thus missed the highest quality of writing. Beerbohm adds the general comment that, though the creative artist is often luminous as a critic, he cannot wholly be trusted.

Thus Beerbohm wrote of Shaw. There is only a passing reference to *Candida* (*Theatres,* 338); and some of the best-known plays, such as *Pygmalion, Heartbreak House,* and *Saint Joan,* came after 1910. Beerbohm's comments raise the central issues about Shaw, and the fact that the judgments are contemporary gives them an urgency, a liveliness which marks the best criticism. Beerbohm found Shaw's plays eminently readable, and usually even better on the stage. Ingenuity in plot and ideas often prevented depth of characterization, and in general Shaw had little interest in emotion or in beauty. Yet Shaw's genius and technical skill commanded Beerbohm's respect. There is occasionally a note of condescension, perhaps inevitable in journalistic reviews, but there is no malice. Although David Cecil remarks (490) that "To the day of his death Max had his knife into Shaw," the reviews of the plays do not support this judgment. Shaw himself must have enjoyed every one of Max's articles about him.

III *The Realists*

Besides Shaw, whose career was unique, the two most important professional dramatists of the period were Henry Arthur Jones (1851-1929) and Arthur Wing Pinero (1855-1934). Beerbohm reviewed fourteen plays by Jones and eleven by Pinero; for *Around Theatres* he selected only his reviews of Jones's *The Lackey's Carnival* and of Pinero's *Iris* and *Letty*. In *The Lackey's Carnival* (1900) Beerbohm found some implausibility in the handling of the valet, but he praised the fresh approach to the life of servants, who because of greater educational opportunities were beginning to reveal themselves as human beings. In reviewing Jones's *Chance, the Idol* (September 13, 1902), Beerbohm said that Jones "of all our regular professional playwrights, is the one whose view of life is least restricted by the conventions of the theatre." This idea is extended in the comment on *Dolly Reforming Herself* (November 7, 1908). Here Jones shows his greatest asset, humor, which is defined as a tolerance for men and women as they are. Shaw, in contrast, has only wit.

Pinero's *Iris* (1901) is a play about a wealthy widow who postpones remarriage because she would thereby forfeit her wealth and thus be forced to share the poverty of her suitor. Beerbohm admires the play because it combines Pinero's usual craftsmanship with greater intellectual honesty than he had exhibited in earlier plays. Nevertheless, Beerbohm refuses to join William Archer in hailing the play as a work of genius. Pinero, he says, has "ever seemed to me a catholic adapter of other men's discoveries." An incidental comment on *The Second Mrs. Tanqueray* in 1900 (*Theatres,* 96–97) had made the same point. The play had first been produced in 1895, and Beerbohm considered it already dated: " . . . it was (not is) no more than a brilliant *pastiche* of Ibsen, grafted on an ordinary commercial melodrama of coincidence . . . its author (for all his cleverness) has yet to betray one symptom of intellectual originality or sincerity."

Despite the progress shown in *Iris,* Beerbohm objects to the formal and unconvincing elegances of diction that blur the idiomatic English necessary in a realistic play. The second review of *Letty* (1903) begins with a parody of Pinero's style and is followed by an analysis of the problems of dramatic dialogue. Characters must seem to talk like real persons; they must all talk like different persons; and, by attention to the cadences of speech, they must talk beautifully. Pinero's ear is defective, as Beerbohm illustrates in a paragraph of examples, such as: "These little differences are invariably settled amicably." In other reviews, Pinero's bookish style is a frequent complaint. Occasionally Beerbohm points out a flaw in plotting. For example, in *The Thunderbolt,* Pinero's solution for a girl of illegitimate birth is marriage to a curate; and, to Beerbohm, Pinero, "good man, has an inveterate weakness for 'the cloth' as a means to a happy ending" (May 16, 1908).

The defects in plays by such competent men as Jones and Pinero made Beerbohm feel strongly that new talent should be encouraged. He looked hopefully toward novelists of reputation, but he was not always pleased with their offerings. Hall Caine's *The Christian*—"a false, garish farrago about life in London"—became only a superficial melodrama on stage (October 21, 1899). Mrs. Humphry Ward's *Eleanor* conveyed no vivid sense of reality (November 8, 1902). Between 1903 and 1908 Beerbohm reviewed three of Somerset Maugham's plays, always kindly, despite some objections to stereotyped characters and situations.[7] Joseph Conrad's *One Day More,* produced by the Stage Society, was praised (1905): Mr. Conrad was "just the sort of person who ought to be coaxed into writing plays." Ian MacLaren, however, whose popular *Beside the Bonnie Brier Bush* was dramatized the same year, had either traduced the character of his fellow Scots or revealed a Scotland "honeycombed with the most insidious forms of maudlin sentimentality" (December 30, 1905).

The plays of John Galsworthy brought high praise, although Beerbohm objected that *Joy* was too inconclusive (September 28, 1907). *Strife,* a play about a strike in which both workers and industrialists lose, he pronounced "a great play" (March 20, 1909). *Justice* (1910) presented a social tragedy with scrupulous fairness, leaving the justifiable implication that the law and the penal system are remediable. Arnold Bennett, whose novel *The Old Wives' Tale* Beerbohm greatly admired in 1908, produced the next year *What the Public Wants.* This play, about a man who marries an intellectual woman, Beerbohm pronounced "one of the best comedies of our time" (May 8, 1909). John Masefield's

The Tragedy of Nan, in Beerbohm's opinion, achieved lyric beauty despite its realistic material (June 13, 1908).

In 1908 Henry James made his last serious attempt to achieve dramatic success with *The High Bid,* a three-act play developed from a one-act curtain-raiser written in 1895 for Ellen Terry, but never performed by her. *The High Bid* is a light comedy about an American woman who buys Summersoft, an English estate, and, in the process, charms the indigent heir into marriage. After production in Edinburgh, the play was brought to London. Beerbohm, long an admirer of James's fiction, found in the play "an inalienable magic" (1909). Most of the review, however, is devoted to James's fiction. An aside in an earlier review of January 28, 1899, implies that Beerbohm saw James's *Guy Domville* in 1895. Without reference to the failure of the play, he thought it "absurd to deny its literary merit." To a present-day reader of *Guy Domville,* this judgment may make charity a vice.

What Beerbohm meant by "realism" in drama might be clearer if such dramatists as Jones and Pinero had produced more satisfactory plays. Repeatedly, he called for more credible characters, situations, and motivations: in short, for less dependence on melodrama and farce. Not everything "real," however, was stageworthy; for, as noted above, Beerbohm found Gorky's *The Lower Depths* boring. Of special importance in realistic drama was dialogue. Each character should speak as an individual; and, by attention to rhythm and idiom, the dramatist could help the actor to speak beautifully as well as truly.

IV *Fantasy and Poetic Drama*

Three playwrights who chose poetic drama and fantasy rather than realism were William Butler Yeats, Stephen Phillips, and J. M. Barrie. In the company of Aubrey Beardsley in 1893, Beerbohm saw Yeats's *The Land of Heart's Desire.* In his reminiscent radio talk of 1954 he describes "the nerveless and inaudible manner" of the performance, and the eerie effect of Yeats's appearance when as author he came before the audience. Not long after this performance, Beerbohm and Yeats had some association as contributors to *The Savoy.*[8] Yeats's mystic intensity bothered Beerbohm, but he respected this quality as pointing, perhaps, to some inadequacy of his own nature. He even journeyed to Dublin to see Yeats's *Countess Cathleen* and a companion piece by Edward Martyn (May 13, 1899). He praised Yeats as a poet and dramatist, and defined his play as an attempt to see whether beauty is possible; he found it in a remoteness "from the stress of common life."

In 1904 Beerbohm welcomed three Irish plays to the London theater as an oasis in the endless desert of drawing-room comedy. The simplicity of production and the poetry of Yeats's lines in *The King's Threshold* pleased him greatly. J. M. Synge's two short plays, *Riders to the Sea* and *In the Shadow of the Glen*, were equally appealing. Beerbohm was convinced that the Irish are naturally adapted to the stage; and Synge's second play, a farce, showed "the utter incapacity" of the Irish to be vulgar. On June 12, 1909, when he saw the two Synge plays again, he found them still charming, but, he reflected, charm rarely accompanies strength. In these comments, Beerbohm is highly conscious of being an outsider. He did not wholly understand the Irish plays, but he valued them because they were new and fresh.

Like a great many of his contemporaries, Beerbohm was impressed by the early success of Stephen Phillips in poetic drama. *Herod*, produced by Beerbohm Tree, was celebrated in two successive articles (November 10 and 17, 1900). In the first, Beerbohm declares that he has no desire to write about so fine a play. In the second, he pronounced the character of Herod "a finely convincing figure." The close of the second act, a scene in which Herod learns that his queen is dead, moved Beerbohm to say: "I have never seen anything more powerful in its irony." In the mannered, rhetorical verse of *Herod* we find it difficult to see a basis for such enthusiasm, but Beerbohm Tree's lavish production may have been influential. Phillips's *Ulysses* was also highly praised (February 8, 1902), but shortly thereafter Beerbohm was annoyed by misuse of his comments about the plays of Phillips in a publisher's promotional booklet. When Phillips's *Aylmer's Secret*, the story of a scientist who fashions a human form, appeared, Beerbohm dismissed it under the caption "A Fantasy Misbegotten" (July 15, 1905).

To Beerbohm, the plays of Barrie must have been more of a problem than those of Shaw. He began by calling Barrie's

Quality Street "the sweetliest, prettiest thing" that he has done (1902). The play is "merely a little fairy story, with characters not pretending to be more than shadows cast by the characters of Miss Jane Austen." Because the actresses who played the old maids were made up to look pretty rather than spinsterly, Beerbohm urged Barrie to demand his rights of the stage manager. From this sophisticated condescension, we turn to this startling sentence later in the same year: "I think *The Admirable Crichton* is quite the best thing that has happened, in my time, to the British stage." This play of the English butler who becomes the natural leader of his aristocratic employers when they are all cast away on a desert island, Beerbohm thinks, has broken new ground: "Mr. Barrie has always been able to amuse us. But this is the first occasion on which he has succeeded in making us also think." Barrie has now been out of fashion so long that the praise seems excessive.

In reviewing Barrie's *Little Mary* Beerbohm made a general judgment even more extreme: "I think his work is on a higher plane than the work of any other living playwright" (October 3, 1903). With *Peter Pan* (1905) he recovered his sense of proportion. *Peter Pan* was the best thing Barrie had done; it revealed Barrie not as a boy who never grew up, but as a child, with a child's dreamlike fancy. In an uncollected review the following week (January 14, 1905), Beerbohm pursued the theme. He doubts whether actual children enjoy such a play as *Peter Pan*. They are "unconscious of being quaint and sweet"; they are not "sensitive to the finer shades of pathos and humor." He recalls once seeing Charles Dodgson (Lewis Carroll) telling a story to a child who listened with a vacant face. Her joy at being released by the storyteller was the vivid memory. Dodgson and Barrie, Beerbohm implies, write for adults. "What children want—no blame to them—is a show with plenty of monsters, demons, noise, and buffoonery."

Thus Beerbohm welcomed the fantasy of Barrie because it touched a quality of feeling quite absent from the literal realism and pseudo-realism which so dominated the theater. Yet there was something false or incomplete about the feeling. In two Continental dramatists—Edmond Rostand (1868–1918) and Maurice Maeterlinck (1862–1949)—Beerbohm found more adult imaginations at work. For him, these playwrights were more approachable than Yeats, more genuine than Phillips, and more satisfying than Barrie.

Rostand's *Cyrano de Bergerac* was presented in London shortly after its triumph in Paris, with the original French-speaking cast, including the great Coquelin in the title role. Writing in 1898, a scant two months after becoming staff reviewer, Beerbohm said that, if the play were not a classic, "it is at least a wonderfully ingenious counterfeit of one, likely to deceive experts more knowing than I." The play is stagy, he concedes, but the young Rostand is a master of stagecraft. Cyrano is a great original character, ingeniously compounded of Caliban, Tartarin, Sir Galahad, and Theodore Hook (an early nineteenth-century wit). So fine is the play in the original French that Beerbohm warns against any attempt at translation. When an English version inevitably appeared (1900), Beerbohm wrote that it was absurd. Cyrano, he now says, is a local type, acceptable in French, but not translatable like such abstract types as Don Quixote or Don Juan. In English, Rostand's rhetoric is ineffective. Two generations later, the praise of the original seems excessive; the condemnation of the translation, too abrupt and unsympathetic.

Beerbohm's response to Rostand's other plays was more moderate. He found *The Fantasticks* (June 2, 1900) similar to Shaw's *Arms and the Man* and, as a satire, suitable for translation. *L'Aiglon* (1901), Rostand's play about Napoleon's son dreaming pathetically of emulating his father's exploits, Beerbohm dismissed as a failure: "Tame eaglet, tame play." Not even the great Sarah Bernhardt saved the title role. The length and scope of the play—fifty characters and four long hours—overshadowed the central story. And, of course, the Napoleon worship, so strong in Paris, was absent in London. One of Beerbohm's last reviews (February 12, 1910) was of Rostand's *Chantecler*, to which he devoted three columns of unalloyed praise.

The poetic plays of Maeterlinck carried Beerbohm as close to lyrical enthusiasm as he ever came. *Pelléas et Mélisande* is a triangle story in which Pelléas falls fatefully in love with his brother's wife, Mélisande. Golaud, the husband, is tormented by jealousy; and, after he kills Pelléas, Mélisande dies. Goland protests, "It is not my fault!" At the end of the play, Mélisande is described as "a poor little mysterious being, like everybody."

This seems a story unlikely to appeal to Beerbohm, yet he wrote on June 25, 1898, that he sat "spellbound and enchanted." The play, he said, "appeals to the sense of beauty and the sense of mystery." Mrs. Patrick Campbell as Mélisande and Forbes-Robertson as the jealous Golaud may have supplied the magic that Maeterlinck's lines now seem to lack, yet when Beerbohm saw another version of the play on March 4, 1899, he spoke of the dramatic power of Maeterlinck and remarked that the characters are "utterly real and human." Reviewing a private production of *Monna Vanna* (June 28, 1902), Beerbohm declared that Maeterlinck was "one of the greatest writers" and "certainly the most loveable writer of his age." *The Blue Bird* prompted the statement that "of all living thinkers whose names are known to me, he has the firmest and widest grasp of truth" (December 18, 1909).

Beerbohm's response to Maeterlinck and his more guarded reaction to Rostand, Yeats, Phillips, and Barrie reveal how strong was the current of romantic feeling which he usually suppressed. His fondness for the Pre-Raphaelites, his liking for Pater and Ruskin, and his appreciation of the poetic side of Wilde and Beardsley are all evidences of a vein of feeling seldom satisfied by the theater of the turn of the century. Beerbohm, who was English enough to distrust feeling, was also wise enough to see its importance. The mood of cool sophistication satisfied part of his nature, and he wore that mask well. But the romantic feeling behind the mask sometimes claimed expression.

V *Shakespeare*

The eight reviews of Shakespearean plays included in *Around Theatres* clearly represent Beerbohm's critical approach. Though in his comments in 1898 on *Macbeth* he censured the cowardliness of Shaw's attacks on a playwright who could not defend himself, Beerbohm himself adopted essentially the same line of attack. For him, as for Shaw, the enemy was not so much Shakespeare as the stodgy tradition that had grown up around his plays. They were so much set apart from the living theater that all too often they were given reverential and undiscriminating praise. When "every head in the auditorium is a heavy casket of reminiscence," it is impossible to get a fresh response to either play or performance (*Theatres,* 9). Beerbohm would therefore like to have fewer performances of such plays as *Macbeth, Romeo and Juliet,* and *Hamlet.* When the Elizabethan Stage Society played the First Quarto *Hamlet* (1900), he applauded the effort: "To me it came almost as a new play." The novelty of *Hamlet* in French, with Sarah Bernhardt in the title role, however, he rejected (1899). The French language, he said, "lacks mystery. It casts none of those purple shadows which do follow and move with the moving phrases of our great poets."

The Tempest Beerbohm welcomed in 1903 for the very reason that it was unhackneyed. The play, he felt, is more artistically compact, and therefore more "modern" than most of Shakespeare. Since Prospero, he theorized, is an autobiographical character, the impersonation should have suggested this. When he turned to *Romeo and Juliet* (1905), Beerbohm, like most critics, found an insoluble difficulty in the youth of the lovers and the maturity of their feelings. Within the limits of this basic disadvantage, he applauded the production; but he thought actors in general ought to be trained to distinguish more carefully between the strictly dramatic lines and those that are poetic ornament.

Beerbohm's uncollected reviews of Shakespeare's plays[9] amplify considerably his skeptical approach. In a comment on *Othello,* he remarks that "Shakespeare has had his day." Of *Lear,* he says that the story is left "barbaric" and cumbered by its primitive origins; yet he concludes that Shakespeare "never did anything more tremendous" than the storm scene. *King John,* which he thought "insufferably tedious" to read, was nevertheless beautifully produced. *Richard III* and *Henry V* he dismissed as "the mere hackwork of genius." *Richard II* was saved only by the part of the king, but from the play Beerbohm quoted lines that sound like a parody of Shakespeare's historical style: "Where is the Earl of Wiltshire? Where is Bagot? What is become of Bushy? Where is Green?" (III, ii, 122-23). *Julius Caesar* (September 15, 1900) seemed to Beerbohm unrelated to anything else by Shakespeare: it is wholly a man's play, and it illustrates the vanity of idealism in practical affairs. Caesar himself is a subordinate character, and he is not made really acceptable. Henry Irving's production of *Coriolanus* Beerbohm deplored: "That Coriolanus is a bad play we are all agreed." Irving he thought inappropriate for the one good part, for Coriolanus is a stupid man. Ellen Terry was wasted in the part of Volumnia.

Shakespeare's comedies fared no better. To Beerbohm, *The Merchant of Venice* is "a particularly sad instance of the way Shakespeare wasted so much of his time." *Twelfth Night,* indeed, has some lovely poetry, but it is "so perfunctory and formless an affair" that it is not even named. *The Merry Wives of Windsor* is "the wretchedest bit of hackwork ever done by a great writer, and [is] by us condoned for the sake of the love we bear him." In Falstaff's "facile coarseness" Beerbohm discerned "hardly one gleam of genuine humour." Gordon Craig's production of *Much Ado About Nothing* was extremely beautiful, but the play itself was unsatisfying: the "merry war" was not really very merry. *Midsummer Night's Dream* was considered in 1900 "the most impressive of all his plays, and the loveliest, and the most loveable"; but in 1908, perhaps because of a poor production, Beerbohm complained that it was dull.

In these numerous comments about Shakespeare (thirty reviews in all), Beerbohm's ideas can hardly be said to have developed. In the later discussions there are the same insistent questions with which Beerbohm began his career as critic. Is the play dramatic? Despite our familiarity with it, does the fresh production create a genuinely fresh response? Does the poetry, however lovely, genuinely contribute to the dramatic effect? Can the actors read the lines appropriately, with due allowance for the verse, and proper accent of its dramatic values? Are the actors properly cast? Is the style of the production intelligent and consistently carried out? These questions are still wholly pertinent; and, like Beerbohm, we must often answer no. To the extent that we recognize the pertinence of these questions, Beerbohm is our contemporary.

VI *Other Revivals*

To the occasional productions of Greek drama Beerbohm brought considerable knowledge of the ancient plays and of the society for which they were written. He had a keen awareness of the difficulties in modern productions of them, but he would not say he enjoyed himself when he was bored. The *Agamemnon* of Aeschylus, presented in Greek in a pleasant open-air theater at Bradfield College, pleased him greatly (1900). He mentions some amateurish slips in the acting, and he questions the decision not to use masks; but these objections are made in a helpful spirit. Later in the same year (November 24), he thought a Cambridge production of the same play made Aeschylus look "ridiculous."

A Bradfield production of Euripides's *Alcestis* (June 25, 1904) left Beerbohm with the feeling that it was Euripides's poorest play, hardly more than a curiosity for a modern playgoer. Earlier in the same month (June 4), he had seen *Hippolytus* in Gilbert Murray's translation. The translation he admired, but the production was only moderately successful. He confessed on January 20, 1906, that *Electra* "bored him beyond endurance." Granville-Barker's production of Aeschylus's *The Persians* (March 30, 1907), though skillful, left the play "as remote as can be." Murray's version of Euripides's *Bacchae* (November 14, 1908) he thought beautiful, but in a modern theater the play was dull. Nevertheless, in comparison to the French playwright Sardou, Euripides is "considerably the nearer man to us."

Gilbert Murray's attempt to modernize Euripides's *Andromache* (1901) was interesting but unsuccessful. "The superstitions that were impressive to us in the old version become definitely absurd in the new. The deeds that were inevitable and pitiable become merely incredible phenomena of brutality." The Christianizing of Andromache makes her grotesque. The division of action into modern acts breaks up the unity of the ancient play. The translation he found literal and uninspired. The actors "were like a hutchful of white rabbits trying to behave like a cageful of lions and failing."

In contrast to the generally adverse response to Greek tragedy, Beerbohm thought the comedies of Aristophanes thoroughly modern and enjoyable. To the Oxford production of *The Clouds*, he devoted two articles (March 4 and 11, 1905); and later (February 20, 1909) he praised the Oxford production of *The Frogs*. Why, he inquired, is Shakespeare always being revived in London, while it is necessary to go to Oxford to see Aristophanes? For any civilized community Aristophanes will always be fresh and contemporary, particularly if the translation is appropriately colloquial.

The great controversy about Ibsen was over when Beerbohm became a drama critic in 1898. As a young man, Beerbohm had heard a good deal about the battle; but, unlike Shaw, he had not been a participant. He was content to accept Ibsen as a fact of history and to approach any revival of his plays in the same spirit that he approached Shakespeare: was the play relevant to a contemporary audience, and if so, was it well performed? The chief article on Ibsen in *Around Theatres* (1906) is the tribute written immediately after Ibsen's death. Ibsen, he thought, was the unlovable type of great man, just as Whitman and Browning represent the lovable type. Ibsen's purpose, despite such plays as *The Doll's House,* was not to reform but, like Mount Vesuvius, to attack and destroy. Even the artistic temperament which Ibsen exemplified he attacked bitterly in one of his late plays, *When We Dead Awaken.*

This estimate of Ibsen had been anticipated by Beerbohm in articles on the English translation of *Ibsen and Björnson* (July 22, 1899) by the Danish critic Georg Brandes; and on William Archer's translation of the plays (July 18, 1903). Archer, like most translators, had an "exaggerated veneration for original authors." As a result, Ibsen's characters are made to talk like books. Edmund Gosse's *Ibsen* prompted additional comment (March 14, 1908): the biography does soften the public image of Ibsen, but he remains unlovable. To Beerbohm, there is a certain comedy in the Scandinavian fondness for their great man, for Ibsen went into voluntary exile because he disliked Scandinavia.

Beerbohm's discussion of specific plays by Ibsen is, however, somewhat more favorable. Writing on W. L. Courtney's *The Idea of Tragedy* (1900), Beerbohm argued that Ibsen had done much to discover the elements of tragedy in common life. Dr. Stockman, in *The Enemy of the People,* illustrates a motive comparable to that of Prometheus. In *The Pillars of Society* (May 18, 1901) Beerbohm found Ibsen "a rattling good playwright." *The Lady from the Sea* (1902), however, bored him with its Ibsenist ideas about women: "Ah! those ideas, how quaint and tedious they have become." *When We Dead Awaken* (February 7, 1903) rightly shows that in the great artist there is some inhumanity, but for Ibsen "To portray is not enough;

he must also preach." Gordon Craig's staging of *The Vikings* Beerbohm commended (April 25, 1903). He was impressed by *Hedda Gabler* (1903) but not by Duse's Hedda. When Mrs. Patrick Campbell played the same part later (March 9, 1907), he remarked: "Did Ibsen ever write a play more masterly than *Hedda Gabler*? If so, I have forgotten it." *Rosmersholm,* in which Florence Kahn appeared (1908), was inevitably appealing, though Beerbohm noted that the realism and the poetry of the play were not perfectly fused.

Two revivals of Oscar Wilde's *The Importance of Being Earnest* led Beerbohm to join in the opinion that the play, first produced in 1895, had proved itself a classic. It had passed the difficult test of treating real life in such a delightful way that even changes of fashion could not affect it. The criticism of the acting (1902) shows how precise a knowledge of the text Beerbohm had. When Miss Prism says that a chapter on the fall of the rupee may be omitted by her charge as too "sensational," the actress has lost effect by substituting "exciting." After a later performance, Beerbohm praised the play as Wilde's best; but he thought that, had Wilde continued to write plays, he would have moved from farce to comedy (December 11, 1909).

Wilde's *Salomé,* banned in 1892 but published in Paris in 1893, was finally produced in London. Beerbohm wrote in 1905 that the play was dramatic but hardly stage worthy. Salomé's lust for John the Baptist, effective when the play is read, arouses physical disgust when represented, particularly if the cardboard stage property simulating John's head is obtrusive, as it was in this production. Sarah Bernhardt, originally intended for the role of Salomé, might have mitigated the effect of this crucial scene; but the "young lady" assigned the role was inept and incongruous.

Toward a miscellany of other revivals Beerbohm was, in general, cool. The conditions under which the plays had originated could not be duplicated; as a result, over-reverence or boredom made the occasions awkward. *Everyman,* the old morality play, Beerbohm saw at his old school on July 27, 1901, and again elsewhere on April 11, 1903; both productions pleased him. John Fletcher's *The Gentle Shepherdess,* he reminds his readers, was a failure on the stage in the seventeenth century; its failure in 1903 was not surprising. As for Congreve's *The Way of the*

World, he thought it, on November 19, 1904, "as dead as a doornail—was never, indeed, alive"; he concedes, however, that it survives as a gallery of characters, and that "every speech is a sharp-cut jewel." T. W. Robertson's *Caste,* an early realistic play (1867), was twice revived (March 25, 1899, and May 3, 1902). Beerbohm, who respected the play as an important achievement in a period of weak dramatic talent, thought it could only be presented on a modern stage as a costume piece. In a single review of July 13, 1901, he briefly treated Racine and Molière. Sarah Bernhardt in *Phèdre* had such great power, he said, that "she almost makes us forget the obsoleteness of Racine." Molière's *Les Précieuses Ridicules,* however, was "as fresh and vital" as when first produced.

For Beerbohm, "tradition" in the theater was a trap for sentimental self-deception. The fact that a play had pleased an earlier audience made it almost certain that a current audience would not really enjoy it but would pretend to do so. As we have seen, there were but few exceptions. Beerbohm expected the theater to speak to him not only as a man of intelligence and taste but also as a man of his own time. Even a revival should be judged on its present merits, not on its importance in theatrical history.

VII *Actors and Production*

Perhaps because Beerbohm knew so many stage people early in life, he never stood in awe of them; indeed, he was often condescending. His frequent use of "mimes" made them sound like lesser people, though he once explained, on September 16, 1905, that the word was convenient simply because it included both actors and actresses. Playfully, he suggested on July 21, 1906, that adulation of stage people was so dangerous that it might well be made a penal offense to invite them to dinner or to publish their articles. More seriously, he thought temperament much more important to an actor's success than intelligence. Repeatedly he said that, as compared with the French, English people had little talent for acting (*Theatres,* 140). Straying once into a seat remote from the stage, he reported (*Theatres,* 427) that the strange sound "Want—pew" finally translated itself into "Want to help you." Actors were not only careless in diction; they were often overconscious of dress and ostentatious in movement. Assuredly, he said (October 19, 1907), a gentleman on taking a seat adjusted his coattails and trousers, "but on the stage some concessions have to be made to effect." Two young American actresses, later eminent, were for the time being deflated. Ethel Barrymore he thought (May 28, 1904) "a fluttering amateur." Billie Burke's nervous mannerisms led him to recommend (May 15, 1909) that she go to a convent, meditate, and observe.

The two great actresses of Beerbohm's day were the Italian Eleanora Duse and the French Sarah Bernhardt. As for Duse's conception of the parts she played (Magda, Paula Tanqueray, Fedora, and Princess George), Duse "has no conception of any one of them. She treats them as so many large vehicles for expression of absolute self." As a personality, she seemed a "great egoistic force . . . overriding, with an air of somber unconcern, plays, mimes, critics, and public. In a man I should admire this tremendous egoism very much indeed. In a woman it only makes me uncomfortable. I dislike it. I resent it. In the name of art I protest against it" (1900). Under the caption "An Hypocrisy in Playgoing" (1903), Beerbohm again protested when Duse played the part of Hedda Gabler in Italian with great critical adulation; even Shaw was enthusiastic. On this occasion Beerbohm confessed that, unlike most of those who praised Duse, *he* did not understand Italian.

In reviewing Sardou's *La Sorcière* (1904), Beerbohm devoted most of his space to Sarah Bernhardt. He developed an analogy between her career and that of the late Queen Victoria, who represented so vast a panorama of recent history: Sarah, he felt, "is still lightly triumphant over time." But he qualifies this praise. In her old parts she can repeat the old effects, but in new parts she merely adapts the old tricks to show herself off: "She, too, after all, is mortal, like the rest of us." When he reviewed Sarah's *Memoirs* (1907), he emphasized her moods, her rages, and the apparent contradiction between her denunciation of capital punishment and her voluntary presence at four executions. Her actions derived from her absolute commitment to emotion for emotion's sake, but this characteristic made her the greatest of living tragediennes.

Ellen Terry's *The Story of My Life* (1908) drew comments about Miss Terry as a person rather than as an actress, though on many previous occasions Beerbohm had praised her acting skill. "She is a woman—a very extraordinary woman—first, an actress afterwards." Her vitality and her sense of the present make her such a great actress, and, in her recollections, such a delightful writer.

On the death of Henry Irving, Beerbohm wrote (1905) a tribute to his long career as the leading British actor. Despite an enumeration of faults, Beerbohm is generous in his praise. Irving, it is true, was deficient in literary sense and often chose to appear in hack work that would give him a big part. He helped to develop the star system, a major obstacle in achieving balanced productions. He could not declaim well, and hence built up his Shakespeare productions as spectacles. Yet his productions of Shakespeare were studious and often splendid. On stage, he had a special magnetism; and, along with his great dignity, he had a sense of fun. When Beerbohm saw Irving in 1895, bound for the ceremony of knighthood at Windsor Castle, he looked very elegant in his carriage, and very bohemian. He was reminiscent of Disraeli; in fact, he and Disraeli might have traded places. When W. H. Pollock's *Impressions of Henry Irving* appeared (1908), Beerbohm wrote that the biography was too worshipful. An adequate biography would show how the early bohemian Irving changed to the pontifical Irving of later years who was egotistical, sometimes cruel, and overanxious to act a part in private life.

The death of Coquelin, the great French actor, Beerbohm thought (1909) "a blow to the whole educated world," though not a misfortune to Coquelin, who died suddenly and without pain. Coquelin in private life was even more robust than he was on the stage. Beerbohm recalls how pleasant it was to see him on holiday at Dieppe. His greatest ambition was to play the title role in Rostand's *Chantecler,* which had just been completed; but death had perhaps saved Coquelin from a humiliating failure.

Like the foibles of actors, the caution and the commercialism of managers were a frequent complaint in Beerbohm's weekly articles. From the Drury Lane Theatre he coined two words: "Druriography" (September 23, 1899), by which he meant the tailoring of plays to fit the stage sets available; and "Druriocracy" (September 29, 1900), the insistence on melodrama long after it had ceased to satisfy playgoers. Instead of bad melodrama like *Quo Vadis* (1900), Beerbohm inquired why managers were not competing for Shaw's new plays. Looking back on June 8, 1901, however, Beerbohm could reflect that the melodrama and farce of twenty years earlier had largely been replaced by comedy. The change was welcome, but it exposed the fact that at least three theaters were too large for the intimate effects of comedy.

When A. B. Walkley asserted that there was no need for a repertory theater, Beerbohm disagreed. He gave special attention to plays produced at the Court Theatre and to those by such groups as the Stage Society, the Playgoers' Club, and the Elizabethan Stage Society. When he served on a committee for the Playgoer's Club, it is true that he found in the scripts submitted for his reading not one scene, not one character worth encouraging (July 14, 1906). Nevertheless, he insisted that new talent must be encouraged and given reasonable opportunity to experiment.

As for staging, Beerbohm found his friend Gordon Craig (Ellen Terry's son) the one really imaginative designer. Beerbohm reminded the English public that Craig was recognized on the Continent long before he was given opportunities in England. And Beerbohm was lavish in his praise of Craig's designs for *Much Ado About Nothing* (May 30, 1903) and for Ibsen's *The Vikings* (April 25, 1903).

VIII *Censors, Critics, and Criticism*

From time to time, Beerbohm commented on the problem of censorship, always in derogatory fashion. The Lord Chamberlain's power of licensing a play for public performance was actually administered by a Mr. Redford, whose judgments were often inconsistent and capricious. When Redford justified some borderline decisions on the subsequent success of the plays concerned, what became of principle? If the introduction of the name of the deity was a sound basis for denying a license, Beerbohm inquired on April 11, 1903, why the Charterhouse production of the old morality play *Everyman* should be permitted. Under the caption "Some Censors" Beerbohm on June 5, 1909, linked together the censorship of one of Shaw's plays, the dean of Westminster's refusal to allow the burial of George Meredith's ashes in the national shrine, and some judgments of Sir Edward Poynter of the Royal Academy. The folly of such official judgments was illustrated by the ease with which they could be circumvented. Shaw could without penalty publish the offending passages in his play; qualified critics could readily dissent from the judgments of the dean of Westminster and Sir Edward Poynter. Plays refused a license for public production could often be presented in "private" performances. When a parliamentary committee recommended a committee of appeal, Beerbohm referred to the proposed committee as a five-headed monster. Like most critics, Beerbohm was concerned with artistic judgment, which was complex and difficult enough without official interference.

Beerbohm's concept of his function as a critic remained essentially impressionistic. The highest type of criticism, he says in *Theatres* (95), is "to translate, through one's own temperament and intellect, the fine work of another man, to cast new lights on its beauties, to reveal hidden things in it, to illustrate and extend its meanings." But critics were unpopular partly because of the traditional dislike of schoolmasters; partly because "all natural things are tainted with unreason" (293). And, though good critics are good for drama, criticism cannot create it.

In an early review of volumes of collected criticism by his contemporaries, William Archer and A. B. Walkley (1899), Beerbohm illustrated very clearly his critical preferences. Though he admired both men, Archer seemed too academic, too eager to find good in everything—in a word, too little prejudiced. William E. Henley roaring oaths, or George Moore "prancing in a forest of mistakes," could occasionally be right in a fresher way. "I like better the opinions of strong, narrow, creative personalities," Beerbohm asserted. Walkley, on the other hand, was a little too scientific, a little too given to remembering what his predecessors had said. He was amusing, but he seemed to despise the theater. On another occasion (July 22, 1905), Beerbohm shrewdly observed that study sometimes diminished a man's power to write well about his enthusiasms.

Beerbohm's preference for the occasional critic, the gifted amateur, is illustrated by his praise of a volume by Arthur Symons (1903), who brought to the theater a definite self. Symons's comments on acting are valuable, in particular, because they rest on "keen and patient observation, made from a sound knowledge of first principles." Symons has creatively expressed the influence of Pater: "Art matters more than life, and form in art more than meaning." Beerbohm himself rejects this view, as well as some errors that stem from it; but he welcomes Symons's criticism as a genuine response.

Like Symons, Beerbohm brought to the columns of *The Saturday Review* a definite self. Unsigned, most of his reviews would be easily identifiable. He remained throughout his twelve years as reviewer the gifted amateur—the man whose business it is to be bored with the second-rate. There is hardly an allusion to the caricatures he was producing at the same time, but his drawing no doubt provided something of the detachment required to do his work about the theater. His first business was to see; his second, to express what he saw. His success is measured by the fact that, no matter how trivial or dull the play may be, Beerbohm's comment brings it once more to attention with a flash of perception and with a memorable turn of phrase.

CHAPTER 4

Retirement: 1910-1956

FROM Genoa southeast to Spezia and beyond, the road winds into the mountains and down to the sea. It is one of the most scenic routes in Europe. Rocky cliffs abound, with here and there a sheltered harbor. In such a spot is Rapallo, twenty miles from Genoa. Behind it rise steep, forested mountains. Along the curve of the shore is a broad promenade, with a façade of hotels and restaurants. To the southwest a squarish peninsula juts into the blue Mediterranean, creating the Gulf of Rapallo. In 1909, Baedeker gave the population of the town as fifty-eight hundred. Even then Rapallo was known as a winter resort, to be reached, of course, by rail. Later guidebooks speak of the parish church with its leaning tower, a medieval *castello,* the church of San Francesco, and seaside resorts which could be reached by carriage or on foot.

In 1907 Beerbohm had visited friends at Santa Margherita, on the peninsula. When he left England with Florence shortly after their marriage in May, 1910, Santa Margherita was their destination. By great good fortune they soon found Villino Chiaro (Bright Cottage), two miles south of the center of Rapallo. From 1910 until his death in 1956 the Villino was home for Beerbohm. The main road, now heavily traveled, was quiet then; and, from a height of three hundred feet, the Beerbohms looked down on the Mediterranean and the curving shore of the Gulf of Rapallo. The Villino was a two-story house. The lower floor was used for storage, and on the second floor were kitchen, bath, and four other small rooms. The paved flat roof was balustraded to serve as patio or deck. Pots of camellias and gardenias added to the charm of olive and orange trees nearby. A small summer house on the roof was later made over into a study for Beerbohm, and eventually a small outbuilding was converted to a *casetta* or guest house.

As at Merton and in London, the study had light blue walls, and above the single bookshelf running along them were hung numerous caricatures. There was a square wooden writing table and an unpainted drawing stand, the latter designed so that Beerbohm could stand as he drew. The other rooms were simply furnished. There was a fireplace in the library, and before it the chair Beerbohm's father had bought for him when he went to Oxford. A convex mirror which once hung in Beerbohm's nursery reflected the room in miniature. In the hall, Beerbohm painted frescoes of the Pre-Raphaelite painters and poets. In his own bedroom, a mural brought together incongruously twelve of Beerbohm's favorite subjects for caricature, among them Henry James, Will Rothenstein, and Rudyard Kipling.[1]

In the early years at Villino Chiaro, the Beerbohms enjoyed an idyllic life. They walked in the olive groves, and they bathed in the sea. Sometimes they read aloud a favorite author like Anthony Trollope. Servants were cheap, and Florence took pleasure in maintaining a clean, orderly, quiet household. Beerbohm himself wrote, drew, and read at leisure. He made no effort to learn Italian, and he seldom visited the local shops in Rapallo. Beerbohm had few visitors in these early years, save for Max's favorite sister Dora. Letters of the time testify to Beerbohm's delight in Italy and to his adoration of his wife. To Will Rothenstein he wrote that she was "absolutely perfect in everything, and adorable. And I am as happy as the day is long."[2]

Marriage brought no disillusionment. Beerbohm called Florence "a perfect darling" in the literal sense, he explained, not in the slang phrase. He teased her with nicknames—the Gazy-bo Girl, Gramnivorous Gertie, the Pittsburgh Virago—but he praised her cooking and housekeeping. In 1911, when he went alone to London to prepare for an exhibition of drawings, he eagerly anticipated his return; and he was overjoyed when she met him at the station in Genoa. In 1913, after he was ill for a time, he bragged to his friend Turner that Florence "made everything run on wheels beautifully." Early in 1914 they were together in London for a few weeks before Florence went alone to visit her family in America. Beerbohm wrote her of witnessing the opening of Parliament. The long description is without a touch of satire. It was as if he had seen the ceremony through her serious eyes: "And after they had passed I found myself with tears in my eyes and an indescribable sadness—sadness for the King—the little King with the great diamonded crown that covered his eyebrows, and with eyes that showed so tragically much of effort, of the will to please. . . ."[3]

Against this background of idyllic leisure and a happy marriage, Beerbohm was doing a good deal of work. The novel *Zuleika Dobson,* begun as early as 1898, was finished early in 1911. Later that year he held an exhibition of drawings in the spring, published the novel in October, and published in November *Cartoons,* an old series exhibited in 1901 at the time of the Boer War. In 1912 came *A Christmas Garland,* a collection of seventeen parodies, nine of them previously unpublished. In 1913 another spring exhibition of drawings was followed in October by publication of *Fifty Caricatures.* For exhibitions of his drawings Beerbohm gave careful attention to proper framing and arrangement. For all books, he was directly concerned with details of design and typography. It is clear that the first years of retirement were busy and productive.

I *World War I*

Beerbohm's feelings about the outbreak of World War I in August, 1914, are clearly recorded in two letters to his friend Reggie Turner. He wrote on September 6 that he was oppressed with "the horror and sadness and absurdity of it." He hoped that Germany would be beaten, but he accurately foresaw that her defeat would probably lead to an even more perilous desire for revenge. He was apprehensive about Russia. With the kind of idealism that animated such men as Rupert Brooke, the poet, Beerbohm observed: "Dear England has behaved with all the fineness one expects of her; and I love to think of her fleet and its magnificent success the world over. . . . Ever since I have lived away from England I have been growing more fond and proud of England as an *idea.* As such, there never has been or will be anything to touch her." The practical difficulties in the way of victory worried him; surprisingly, he thought the new Pope Benedict might, by a papal bull against Germans and Austrians as responsible for the war, compel their governments to end it. In December Beerbohm contemplated returning to England. He wanted to see his family and "to feel that I shall not have been away during the whole of England's hour of need." The lapse into the idiom of the day is perhaps indicative of how deeply Beerbohm felt involved. The war was too vast, too catastrophic, to be expressed in characteristic Beerbohm style.[4]

In the spring of 1915 the Beerbohms did return to England, where they remained until the war was over. Beerbohm thought of doing some kind of clerical war work, but nothing came of this plan. The government asked him to do some drawings for use in propaganda; but, because he doubted his ability for such work, he suggested that Raemakers, the Dutch cartoonist, was better qualified. Lacking any regular employment, Beerbohm adapted his Italian routine to wartime England. For nearly two years he and Florence lived with the Will Rothensteins at Far Oakridge in Gloucestershire, some eighty miles west of London. At first they stayed in the Rothenstein home, later at a guest house nearby. Rothenstein vividly recalls the pleasure of renewing the friendship begun in 1893. With the Rothensteins, Beerbohm read aloud some of his writings, exhibited his drawings, and invented a sonnet game in which he and Will wrote alternate lines. Though the countryside was beautiful, Beerbohm made no concessions to it. He walked as little as possible, and dressed as if he were in London—gloves, spats, stick, and all. When a nearby hayrick caught fire, the farmer was astonished to see a neatly gloved volunteer joining the farm hands.[5]

It was the illness and death of Herbert Beerbohm Tree that drew the Beerbohms to London. Shortly after returning from a government mission to America, Herbert had a fall in which he injured his leg. An operation, apparently successful, was followed by a fatal heart attack. Nine months later, Beerbohm's mother died. As the man of the family, Max took charge of the practical details in these situations. The mass of papers Herbert left, in particular, required tact as well as time. A memorial volume was thought appropriate, and Max undertook to collect material for it and to edit it. Much correspondence was involved, and Beerbohm himself wrote the sketch "From a Brother's Standpoint." Partly because of this project, the Beerbohms did not return to Rapallo immediately after the Armistice (November 11, 1918), but remained in England until late the following year. Even so, work on the proofs of the book compelled Beerbohm to make a special trip to England a few weeks later.

Outwardly, the war years had been idle and futile for Beerbohm. Yet during this period he had done most of the drawings that were to appear in *Rossetti and His Circle* (1922), usually considered his best work in caricature; he had completed *Seven Men* (1919), his volume of fictional sketches; and he had written some of the best essays for his fourth collection, *And Even Now* (1920). "Hosts and Guests," "Servants," and "A Clergyman" are three of these. The renewal of old friends in England was undoubtedly stimulating, and he also met new people. In 1917, for instance, he met Lytton Strachey, whose *Eminent Victorians* was so great a literary event the following year. Later Beerbohm and Strachey became better acquainted, and in 1943 Strachey was the subject of the Rede lecture which Beerbohm delivered at Cambridge.

II *The 1920's*

The 1920's were probably the years in which Beerbohm enjoyed his widest popularity. A Collected Edition of his works, in ten volumes, appeared between 1922 and 1928. There were numerous editions both in England and in America of his early collections of essays, and seven editions of *Zuleika Dobson*. Though the first collections of caricatures were not reissued, there were successful exhibitions of new work in London in 1921, 1923, and 1925. Besides the *Rossetti and His Circle* (1922), already mentioned, Beerbohm published three other collections of drawings: *A Survey* (1921), *Things New and Old* (1923), and *Observations* (1925). In 1928 he published *A Variety of Things,* a collection of twelve pieces which rounded out the collected edition; and in the autumn he arranged an exhibition called "Ghosts," drawings of one hundred and nine persons he had known. In July, 1930, the University of Edinburgh conferred an honorary degree. Beerbohm wrote to Turner of the rounds of cheers for certain other venerable recipients of degrees and for "the (hang it all, not quite so) venerable me."[6]

There was, to be sure, an outcry in 1921 over an anti-Labour cartoon. Beerbohm depicted a prospective Labour minister of education scoffing at a poet who asked for aid. The drawing was dedicated to young poets who "imagine that under the domination of Labour the liberal arts might have quite a decent chance." When *The Daily Herald* scolded Beerbohm for his vulgarity, Beerbohm replied that, though he had never been called vulgar before, vulgarity has its uses. He expressed the hope that Labour leaders would see his drawing and be reminded that "the well-being of skilled and manual workers is not quite all that matters."[7]

A more serious objection was made to Beerbohm's exhibition of 1923, which included several drawings of the royal family. "Angel Edward" depicted the late monarch as a fat angel playing a harp in heaven. Another, "Long Choosing and Beginning Late," showed Mr. Edward Windsor in a future Communistic England, married to Miss Flossie Pearson, the daughter of his landlady, who gives her new son-in-law a fine "character."[8] Newspapers attacked these drawings and others in the series as "an offence to good taste" and as "a dastardly attack on Royalty." Beerbohm, who accepted the public verdict, suggested that the offending pictures be removed. In a letter released to the press, he told the managers of the Leicester Galleries: "No question of principle is involved. The question is one of taste merely, and I cannot strike a dignified attitude and say to the public in solemn tones, 'My taste, believe me, is perfect.' " The drawings, he continued, were mere fantasy, with no intended unkindness or disloyalty; if they were likely to be misunderstood, they should be removed.[9] The preface to *Things New and Old* makes similar reference to the drawings objected to, which were omitted from that volume.

In the autumn of 1924, Florence made another trip to America, leaving Beerbohm alone at Rapallo. The following March he went to London to arrange his next exhibition of drawings. Besides seeing old friends, such as Arnold Bennett, Beerbohm met the Sidney Schiffs,[10] who on many subsequent occasions were hosts to the Beerbohms when they were in England. In 1927, Will Rothenstein came to Rapallo and took Beerbohm to see the German poet and playwright, Gerhart Hauptmann. Hauptmann could speak no English, Beerbohm no German; but the two men liked each other. Hauptmann's secretary, Elisabeth Jungmann, who acted as interpreter, was lively and warm; and she soon became a frequent visitor at Villino Chiaro. The friendship continued in England during World War II, and on the death of Florence Beerbohm in 1951, Elisabeth became companion and housekeeper; during Beerbohm's last illness, they were married.

In 1928, when another exhibition brought Beerbohm to London, Beerbohm called on his old friend Henry Arthur Jones, the dramatist, then in his last illness. At Rothenstein's, Beerbohm met students of the Royal College of Art, of which Rothenstein became principal in 1920. A number of celebrities were, as usual, in the Rothenstein circle, and one of them was Ramsay MacDonald. MacDonald had served briefly as prime minister in 1924, and was to hold that office again from 1929 to 1935. Though a Labour leader, he had much of the patrician manner, an eloquence that recalled Gladstone, and a genial disposition. He and Beerbohm took to each other at once. On various occasions MacDonald sought out Beerbohm's company, and he once invited him and the Rothensteins to lunch at Chequers, the country residence of the prime minister.[11]

III *The 1930's*

Life in Rapallo was interrupted by several trips to London. For Beerbohm, Florence's stage appearances were important incidents. In 1931, she played the lead in Pirandello's *The Life I Gave You,* a subtle and demanding part; in 1935, she took the role of Aase, the mother in *Peer Gynt;* in the same year, she had a minor role in an Oxford production of *Richard II*. Though many considered Florence a stilted, old-fashioned actress of little talent, Beerbohm saw her dramatic roles through a haze of affection and delighted in such recognition for her as these performances conferred.[12]

During much of 1935 the Beerbohms lived in Tavistock Square in the Bloomsbury area near the British Museum. The essay "From Bloomsbury to Bayswater"[13] records Beerbohm's rather unflattering impressions of Bloomsbury. He did not enjoy its architecture, its reputation as a center for the intelligentsia (in his view, a mental underworld), and the slovenly appearance of the people. As a gesture of disapproval, he bought a Carthusian school tie of bright crimson, salmon pink, and royal blue. Inwardly, he recalled Chelsea, the more cheerful artistic center of his youth. In 1936, when he was again in London, he lived more happily in Bayswater, a residential district west of Marble Arch, not far from the Hyde Park Place of his Oxford vacations. In

Bayswater, he thought, the air was purer and the people happier.

By the mid-1930's radio had become important for most people in England, as well as in America. The Beerbohms took it up belatedly, but with unexpected enthusiasm. From London, Beerbohm wrote Turner that the British Broadcasting Corporation (BBC) was "a wonderful triumph of variety and soundness." He had been listening to Shaw, to Chesterton, and to D. S. MacColl, an art critic and former colleague on *The Saturday Review*. MacColl had the best voice, he thought. Next to him was King George V, and next to him Gracie Fields, the music-hall singer. In October, Mr. Moray McLaren of the BBC invited Beerbohm to provide a talk on London in a program called "Revisited." Beerbohm replied with a blend of excitement and caution. He wanted a "bribe" of ninety pounds; but, before he would agree to "radiate," he asked for a three-minute test of his voice, to be monitored by Mr. McLaren and by Florence.[14]

The test, duly arranged for at a hotel with an appropriate Edwardian decor, was very successful. The first broadcast, December 29, brought a great deal of fan mail, which Beerbohm enjoyed. Two other talks followed on April 19 and July 2, 1936. For these broadcasts Beerbohm rehearsed carefully, going over his manuscript aloud to get precise timing and rhythm. The first talk, "London Revisited," and a reading of his essay "A Crime," were issued as a recording, one unhappily no longer available. Beerbohm's soft but precise voice is courteously reserved, yet intimate. The charms of vanished London are affectionately described: the Piccadilly goat who lived near the home of the Duke of Cambridge; the horse-driven barouches, hansoms, and phaetons; the lost façades of familiar squares—Saint James's, Berkeley, Portman, and Kensington. There are harsh, rasping references to modern London; but they are not offensive, even if the listener is disposed to challenge them. The mind and taste behind that cultivated voice are, he feels, entitled to opinions, even uncomfortable ones.

IV *World War II*

The Munich crisis in the autumn of 1938 once more made it advisable for the Beerbohms to return to England. Nine years passed before they could go back to Rapallo. Their friends Sydney and Violet Schiff offered them a cottage on the grounds of their country house at Abinger, near Dorking, thirty miles south of London. Personal griefs combined with public anxieties. In two months, three persons close to Beerbohm died: Viola, his favorite niece; Reggie Turner, his close friend since the first year at Oxford in 1890; and Constance, the half-sister who for many years had managed the Beerbohm household in London.

Life at Abinger was as pleasant as bad times permitted, and Beerbohm took frequent trips elsewhere. A little paper, *The Abinger Chronicle,* was started by some literary friends, and to it Beerbohm made several contributions. Elisabeth Jungmann, who had a government position during the war, knew the Sydney Schiffs and occasionally visited Abinger. In July, 1939, a knighthood was conferred; and Sir Max Beerbohm, despite his jibes at royalty and titles, was pleased. In 1942 he gave two radio talks, one on old music halls (January), in which he ventured to sing some of the old songs, and another (September), in which he attacked the vulgarity of modern advertising. In honor of his seventieth birthday, August 24, the Maximilian Society was inaugurated with a testimonial dinner in London. In November, Oxford conferred an honorary degree. In 1943 he delivered the Rede lecture at Cambridge, a tribute to Lytton Strachey, who had died in 1932. In 1945 his old college at Oxford, Merton, made him an honorary fellow. Life was easy for no one during these years, and there was a special strain for those not directly involved in some part of the war effort. The honors that came to Sir Max must for that reason have been particularly welcome.

The pleasant life at Abinger was abruptly terminated by a flying bomb in August, 1944, which demolished the cottage occupied by the Beerbohms. Unruffled, Sir Max superintended the loading of baggage into a limousine that took him and Florence to nearby friends. For some time they had no settled residence. In November, Sydney Schiff died; and in February, 1945, Sir William Rothenstein, whose friendship with Beerbohm had begun at Oxford in 1893. Rothenstein had known two generations of artists in England and on the Continent. He had been knighted in 1931, had long directed the Royal College of Art, and had been active in the planning of an art record of the war. Appropriately, it was the old friend, Sir Max, who delivered the memorial address at Saint Martin's-in-the-Fields at Trafalgar Square. Of Rothenstein he said: "His spirit will remain. But that fine brain of his, and that fine heart of his, have ceased their work."[15]

The end of the war found the Beerbohms in precarious circumstances. The legacy from Turner in 1938, equal to some fifteen thousand dollars, had not been sufficient to supplement the meager earnings from occasional articles and broadcasts. Even if it had been economically feasible, remaining in England was not an attractive prospect. Postwar London seemed uglier than ever, and few of the old friends were left. War feeling had died down in Italy, and there seemed to be no reason why the Beerbohms should not return to their beloved Rapallo. In April, 1947, Florence went first to Villino Chiaro, which she found unharmed. Meanwhile, Beerbohm journeyed to North Ireland, where his sister Agnes lived with her husband's people. Except for Max, she was the last of the family, and six months later, she died. After setting Villino Chiaro to rights, Florence returned to England, and together the Beerbohms made their last trip to Rapallo at the end of September. They must have realized that they would not see England again. Max was seventy-five; Florence, sixty-nine. Until her death in 1951, they were never again separated.

In the years during the wars, especially the nine years from 1938 to 1947, the Beerbohms were naturally thrown much with Max's English friends. Florence was at a disadvantage. She was away from her own home, for how long she could not tell; and she was subject to the inconveniences and strains of wartime England. Max's friends, deprived of his company when he lived in Italy, wanted to make the most of him now that he was in or near London again. Florence did not fit in with them, any more than she had in the Beerbohm household at 48 Upper Berkeley Street. There are unpleasant stories: she interrupted him; she left the table in protest at a second bottle of wine; she even tore up an impromptu caricature. Mrs. Sydney Schiff, with whom the Beerbohms stayed during much of the war, thought Florence dramatized herself and displayed inflexible attitudes. Once she would have nothing to do with an unmarried servant girl about to have a child.[16] In Max's eyes, these fits of temper were trifles. When in 1947 he wrote her that he was at last ready to go back to Rapallo, she wrote from the Villino that she did a little dance on the terrace. Max recorded the scene in a lighthearted caricature.

Florence's stage career adds an element of mystery to her character and personality. Her early success in plays of Ibsen does not fit with her shyness offstage. The suggestion that she was seriously considered for such parts as Wilde's Salomé and Shakespeare's Cleopatra is hard to associate with her conventional and puritanical standards of conduct. Her return to the stage in 1931, after twenty years' absence, in a Pirandello part designed for Duse suggests a psychological subtlety that would belie her reputed lack of humor. Perhaps when she and Max were alone together, she was at her best, adapting to their companionship something of the imagination and intelligence she brought to her stage roles. Max, at least, seems to have thought so.

V *Postwar*

The return to Rapallo found Beerbohm unable to do any sustained work. He and Florence kept much to themselves, as before. To escape the heat of the summers, they spent some time in an inexpensive hotel at a mountain resort above Rapallo. There were numerous callers, for Max was not only a celebrity but, as he said, "a link with the past." Two visitors were the Americans Thornton Wilder and Edmund Wilson. Beerbohm found Wilder especially interesting, though Wilson monopolized the conversation.

When a visitor called at the Villino, Florence usually met him and took him to the terrace. There Max, carefully dressed and prepared to act his part, awaited. The talk had a touch of formality, yet Max had never been a monologist. "Tell me," he would say in prelude to polite questions about the activities of younger men and their acquaintances. Their inquiries, in turn, about Wilde, Beardsley, and the subjects of his many caricatures, would bring out anecdotes and dry wit. Once asked if Frank Harris ever told the truth, he replied: "Sometimes, don't you know—when his invention flagged."[17]

Florence's health declined, and she was subject to fits of depression which she could not wholly conceal. On one of Elisabeth Jungmann's visits, Beerbohm recorded her address, and she promised to come at once whenever she was needed. In January, 1951, when he did send for her, Elisabeth arrived only three hours after Florence's death. Elisabeth arranged for the cremation, and a few days later she sat in the boat with Max as the gardener rowed them out to drop into the sea the urn containing Florence's ashes.

It seems to have been silently understood by all three that, after Florence's death, Elisabeth would take care of Max. She had seen Florence's decline, and for a long time she had wanted him to have the kind of care she knew she could give him. She was a mature woman, even in 1927, when in the company of Hauptmann she first met Max. She had a liveliness that Florence lacked; and, without any notable jealousy in Florence, she and Max had been good companions for more than twenty years. After Florence's death, it was Elisabeth who greeted the guests, warned them if he was feeling tired, and helped him to display himself to best advantage. As time went on, Elisabeth became nurse as well as companion and housekeeper; when his rest was disturbed, as it often was by nightmares, Elisabeth came to his room to quiet him, as she might have a sick child.

VI Mainly on the Air *(1946)*

Beerbohm's only book in the postwar years, *Mainly on the Air,* is almost wholly reminiscent. Besides "London Revisited," five other broadcasts were included in the collection. "Advertisements" rather acidly rejects the blandishments of modern commercialism. "Speed" is a pessimistic speculation on the changes brought by the passion for rapid transportation. This essay opens with an unexpectedly favorable recollection of W. E. Henley, the great yea-sayer of the 1890's. "A Small Boy Seeing Giants" has already been drawn upon for its record of Beerbohm's early sight of Gladstone and other parliamentary figures. "Music Halls of My Youth" introduced snatches of many of the old songs, which in the broadcast Beerbohm sang with gusto. "Playgoing" commented on the rise in respectability of the stage through the development of actor-managers, of whom Herbert Beerbohm Tree was a distinguished example.

The eight broadcasts added in the posthumous edition of 1958 were almost wholly about persons Beerbohm had known in his youth: Nat Goodwin, the American actor who lived much in

England; Marie Lloyd, a music-hall singer; George Moore, the Irish novelist; Sir Desmond MacCarthy, whom Beerbohm considered one of the best talkers he ever knew; the elder son of Henry Irving, whom he met at Oxford; and W. B. Yeats as the young poet and dramatist of the Celtic revival. "Hethway Speaking" creates a mythical character who delights in trivial reminiscences of Meredith, Swinburne, Carlye, and William Morris in a manner that parodies all literary small talk. "An Incident" describes a meeting with Henry James, and a polite refusal to accompany the novelist to an art gallery; Beerbohm wanted, instead, to read James's recently published story, "The Velvet Glove."[18] This final broadcast was put on the air on June 14, 1956, nearly a month after Beerbohm's death. To have known that from beyond the grave he was testifying to a lifelong delight in James would have pleased Max greatly.

VII *S. N. Behrman*

Major events of 1952 and the three following years were the visits of S. N. Behrman, the American dramatist. Like many literate Americans, Behrman had enjoyed since early youth the essays and drawings of Beerbohm. He knew that Beerbohm had lived in retirement in Rapallo since 1910, but in various trips to Italy Behrman hesitated to intrude. It was Beerbohm himself who wrote to Behrman, expressing pleasure in one of the American's writings. An exchange of letters led to Behrman's first visit in 1952. Beerbohm and Elisabeth Jungmann were spending part of the summer in the mountains above Rapallo, and Behrman describes vividly his wild trip by taxi, his meeting with Miss Jungmann, the carefully staged entrance of Max, and the luncheon conversation.

Forewarned by Elisabeth that Max did not like "listeners who never talk and talkers who never listen," Behrman asked many questions about Shaw. As a reward, Max's elaborately "improved" copy of Archibald Henderson's early biography of Shaw was displayed.[19] In it, portraits of Shaw are turned into caricatures, and pedantic notes are added, parodying the overreverent style of Henderson.

Behrman's second meeting with Beerbohm, at Villino Chiaro, resulted in a lively and detailed description of the house as it then was. Beerbohm reminisced about his trip to America in 1895, about Wilde, and about Kipling. The long series of attacks on Kipling, Beerbohm half regretted. Kipling, he thought, had been false to his very great genius; and Beerbohm had felt he had to attack him. But once, when he had seen Kipling at a London club, he had had the impulse to go to him and say: "Mr. Kipling, I admire you. . . . If I have written harshly of you, it is because I do not believe you are living up to the possibilities of your genius." The friendly gesture was never made, and Max was sorry.[20]

Behrman made several other visits to Villino Chiaro. Beerbohm's talk, a combination of anecdote, literary opinions, and annotation of his own writings and drawings, is convincing evidence of how alert Beerbohm's mind was when he was past eighty. He recalled precisely how the sudden news of Ibsen's death in 1906 forced him to devote a reluctant evening composing an article about the dramatist's career. As in one of his radio talks, Beerbohm sang for Behrman some of the old music-hall songs. He was pleased to recall Henry James's approval of the parody, "The Mote in the Middle Distance." Caricatures in the volumes of 1907 and 1925 drew discriminating comments on the drawings themselves and on the political and literary figures presented. A drawing of Winston Churchill he thought very poor. "I never succeeded with Winston," he added.[21]

During Behrman's last visit to the Villino, Beerbohm illustrated a story about Oscar Wilde's brother Willie by drawing profiles of the two. These "scratches," as Beerbohm called them, are reproduced in Behrman's volume (290); and they show that at eighty-three Beerbohm's hand had not lost its sure touch. At about this time, Beerbohm was also stimulated to do a last bit of writing. An American collector had secured several nonconsecutive sample sheets of a special edition of *The Happy Hypocrite,* designed by Bruce Rogers, but never brought to completion. The collector brought the sheets to Beerbohm as interesting souvenirs, hoping that the author would inscribe them. Beerbohm kept them for some time and eventually returned them with this note: "Here is the book that you left with me. I have dared to amend, here and there, what seemed to me a lack of continuity in the narration."[22] These impromptu bits of drawing and writing, Mr. Behrman believes, are the last bits of creative work attempted by Beerbohm. It is characteristic that they were done just for the fun of it.

VIII *Death*

The end came quietly, but slowly. On March 26, after an attack of rheumatic asthma, Beerbohm was taken to a hospital in Rapallo. Warned by his doctor that he might not recover, Beerbohm said to Elisabeth: "What do you think of the idea of getting married?" She replied: "I adore you more than anything else in the world. I think it *is* a good idea."[23] He must have known that this would be her reply, and he was pleased. All his oldest friends and closest relatives were dead. Elisabeth knew his wishes; and, as his wife and widow, she could speak with authority. The marriage would assure that his small property and any income from his books would be some recompense for her years of devotion beyond price. On April 20 the ceremony was performed by the mayor of Rapallo.

The next weeks were full of those sufferings which are a trial to the strong and agony to the weak. There were fits of asthma, bed sores, and a heightened sensitivity to the slightest friction. Swinburne's lines in "The Garden of Proserpine" came often to Beerbohm:

> From too much love of living,
> From hope and fear set free;
> We thank with brief thanksgiving
>   Whatever gods may be
> That no life lives forever;
> That dead men rise up never;
> That even the weariest river
>   Winds somewhere safe to sea.

Elisabeth was his greatest comfort, and on May 19 he died as he slept, holding her hand. On May 22 there was a funeral at the village church. After cremation, Beerbohm's ashes were sent to England, where they were interred with ceremony at St. Paul's Cathedral on June 29. His eighty-fourth birthday was then two months distant.

CHAPTER 5

Later Writings

ONE of Beerbohm's purposes in retiring from *The Saturday Review* was to complete his novel *Zuleika Dobson*. This he did promptly, and it was published with great success in 1911. In the following year, *A Christmas Garland* brought together eight old parodies and nine new ones. In 1919 Beerbohm collected in *Seven Men* five fictional sketches linked together by his own presence in each situation. In the same year he was editing and contributing an autobiograpical sketch to a memorial volume for his half-brother, Herbert Beerbohm Tree. A fourth collection of essays, *And Even Now*, followed in 1920. A ten-volume collected edition, 1922-28, included *Around Theatres*, a selection of about a third of the dramatic criticisms published in *The Saturday Review*. In 1928 *A Variety of Things* brought together a dozen items, of which only four are work of the postwar years; the volume was the tenth and last of the collected edition. The successful radio talks of later years led to the publication of *Mainly on the Air* in 1946; the "Other Things" in this volume included three magazine essays of the 1940's. A posthumous edition of *Mainly on the Air* added eight radio talks and the lecture on Lytton Strachey delivered in 1943. Besides these collected writings there are a dozen essays, most of them brief and slight; five reviews of books that had some special interest for Beerbohm; more than twenty brief notes to new editions of his own works or to volumes written by friends; and a dozen or so letters to the editor. *Max's Verse* (1963) contained eighty-four items, many of them previously unpublished.

In these later writings of Beerbohm there is no line of development, no logical sequence. After 1928 the impulse to write came seldom; what Beerbohm wrote is limited in scope and almost fragmentary in substance. Yet, as will appear, the style did not falter. Though chronology will shed less light than it usually does in reviewing an author's work, it will be simplest to describe the later work in approximately the order in which it was published.

I Zuleika Dobson *(1911)*

Beerbohm's love affair with Oxford began even before he went there in 1890, and the idea of writing an Oxford novel occurred to him perhaps as early as 1898. By 1901, he was thinking about a publisher; in 1902, he commented on the difficulties of writing a serious novel about Oxford, and mentioned the farcical *The Adventures of Mr. Verdant Green* as the best Oxford fiction thus far.[1] The obvious difficulty, he pointed out, was the absence of women—a difficulty overcome in the very title of his own novel. After reaching Italy in 1910, Beerbohm must have turned almost at once to the incomplete manuscript. Early in 1911 it was finished, and the following October the novel appeared. It was enthusiastically received. To the reading public Max was still familiar as the lively critic of *The Saturday Review* and as the caricaturist whose recent exhibition had attracted attention.

In later years, *Zuleika Dobson* became one of those special books, not central in a syllabus of the English novel, but highly esteemed by readers who discover it. No synopsis of this famous story ever makes it sound very appealing or impressive. The plot is deliberately preposterous. Zuleika Dobson, a young woman who has had a brilliant success as a performer of magic tricks, comes to Oxford to visit her grandfather, the Warden of Judas College. Driving from the station to the College, she catches a glimpse of the young Duke of Dorset, a student at Judas. That evening the Duke is a dinner guest at the Warden's home, where he immediately falls in love with Zuleika. The Duke's spontaneous love for Zuleika is hopeless, since she can never love a man who abases himself before her. When he enumerates his titles—fourteenth Duke of Dorset, Marquis of Dorset, Earl of Grove, Earl of Chastermaine, Viscount Brewsby, Baron Grove, Baron Petstrap, and Baron Wolock—and the many estates Zuleika would share with him, her only reply is: "I think you are an awful snob." The Duke, having been demeaned by falling in love at all, and even more by being refused, forms the idea of dying for his love: "Death was the one true bridal." It even seemed to him that by dying for Zuleika he might cause her to love him: "He saw her bending over his tomb, in beautiful curves, under a starless sky, watering the violets with her tears."[2]

At the boat races the Duke tells Zuleika his resolve. She does not take him seriously, but that night at a meeting of the Junta, the Duke's exclusive club, the other members do. They, like the Duke and all other undergraduates in Oxford, have fallen irretrievably in love with Zuleika. Like the Duke, they all vow to die for her. After a concert on the same evening, the Duke renews his suit and reconsiders his intention to die for Zuleika; she calls him a miserable coward. A moment later she calls him from an upstairs window; and, when he approaches, she empties a jug of water in his upturned face.

Next morning she sends a note of apology for her "idiotic practical joke." The Duke composes a reply, indicating that his profession of love and his resolution to die for her had also been jokes. At just this point a telegram comes from the Duke's estate: "Deeply regret inform your grace last night two black owls came and perched on the battlements remained there through night hooting at dawn flew away none knows whither awaiting instructions". (XIV, 217). This occurrence, as the Duke had told Zuleika, is the traditional warning that the holder of the title is about to die. The tradition cannot be challenged. The Duke telegraphs his reply: "Prepare vault for funeral Monday."

Having had no answer to her apology, Zuleika calls on the Duke at lunchtime. She confesses that she really loves him and releases him from his promise to die for her. When he shows her the telegram about the owls, she faints. When she recovers (rather quickly), she accepts the inevitability of his death and departs. That afternoon the Duke makes his way to the river, splendidly arrayed in his costume as Knight of the Garter. When rain threatens to spoil his robes, he feels he cannot wait until the end of the races, as he had planned. He plunges into the river shouting "Zuleika." He is followed at once by hundreds of undergraduates. So amazed are the spectators that it is some time before the disaster is realized. Zuleika herself must explain the tragedy to her grandfather, the Warden of Judas. He agrees that she had better leave Oxford at once, returning later, perhaps, "but not in term time." Next day, by special train, Zuleika departs for Cambridge.

How did Beerbohm sustain interest in so preposterous a story, and why? Both questions can be answered if the novel is regarded as a caricature in fantasy. Just as a caricature bears recognizable relation to reality, no matter how great the exaggeration, so the story of Zuleika reflects real life in the very act of distorting it. To begin with, the antique railway station, the Broad, the portals of Balliol and Trinity, the Ashmolean, Blackwell's bookshop, the Sheldonian, and even the grim busts of Roman emperors which adorn it, all give assurance of literal reality. The beauty of Oxford is recurrently evoked. The Duke looks out his window the morning after he met Zuleika:

> Some clock clove with silver the stillness of the morning. Ere came the second stroke, another and nearer clock was striking. And now there were others chiming in. The air was confused with the sweet babel of its many spires, some of them booming deep, measured seqences, some tinkling impatiently and outwitting others which had begun before them. (IV, p. 39)

The narrator, at midnight, pretends that he is a disembodied spirit:

> I floated out into the untenanted meadows. Over them was the usual coverlet of white vapour, trailed from the Isis right up to Merton Wall. The scent of these meadows' moisture is the scent of Oxford. Even in hottest noon, one feels that the sun has not dried *them*. Always there is moisture drifting across them, drifting into the Colleges. It, one suspects, must have had much to do with the evocation of what is called the Oxford spirit—that gentlest spirit, so lingering and searching, so dear to them who as youths were brought into ken of it, so exasperating to them who were not. (XII, 189)

It is all very sentimental, but between the lines is a disarming smile.

Against these last enchantments of the Middle Age—the phrase is Matthew Arnold's, introduced at the end of Beerbohm's first paragraph—how contemporary is the theme of the story. The Duke of Dorset is the epitome of ancient privilege at the very time when such privilege was being seriously challenged. Instead of trying to represent the political battles by which rank and hereditary rights were undermined in the quarter century before World War I, Beerbohm puts before us a more insidious and dangerous challenge: the New Woman. Aggressive, rational rather than traditional, Zuleika is not impressed by the Duke's titles and estates. In 1885, Henry James (Beerbohm's favorite novelist) had treated seriously the same theme: Isabel Archer, in *The Portrait of a Lady*, refused Lord Warburton; and, though that nobleman had too much common sense to throw himself into the river because of thwarted love, he seems to have led but a sad life ever after. The feminine frills and furbelows of Zuleika's Edwardian costumes merely accentuate her independence as a New Woman.

Not only does the story caricature the New Woman; it caricatures the theme of romantic love, which had its most extreme statement in the Pre-Raphaelite paintings and poems and in the Wildean esthetic movement which preoccupied the 1890's. The Duke's love for Zuleika, and that of every other undergraduate, is spontaneous and complete. There is no room for it to grow, and so the perfect expression of it is death. In Beerbohm's own infatuation for Cissie Loftus, begun while he was at Oxford and she was a fifteen-year-old music-hall singer, there was an ardor that closely paralleled the Duke's. Beerbohm adored Cissie not as a living and marriageable girl, but as an Idea. In a letter to Turner, Beerbohm imagines how beautifully he could mourn over Cissie's grave if she were to die. But her use of rouge and her singing of slightly vulgar songs wounded his sensibilities.[3] In the same way, the Duke, when Zuleika called him a snob instead of melting into his arms, hardly considered whether he *was* a snob; it was Zuleika who had betrayed his idea of romantic love. The sheeplike adoration of the other undergraduates amusingly suggests that, despite brilliant scholarship and surface sophistication, there was a fundamental immaturity in their relations with women.

Other features of Oxford life are deftly caricatured. Zuleika's grandfather is reduced to donnish formality. He waits for her on the station platform "aloof and venerable . . . an ebon pillar of tradition . . . in his garb of old-fashioned cleric." Before Zuleika comes down for dinner, the Warden explains that she "devotes her life to good works." The Duke's familiarity with her career as entertainer surprises the Warden. He had forgotten that "she had achieved some fame in the outer world." Toward the end of the novel, the Warden is mystified by the failure of the students to assemble in the dining hall. Even the sub-Warden does not dare to explain that all the young men have thrown themselves into the river for love of his granddaughter. Later, when Zuleika explains what has happened, he at first thinks that only the boys of his own college have drowned themselves, obviously a tragic disaster. When Zuleika makes clear that *all* the undergradutes of the university have died for her, the Warden is actually relieved: "This changes the aspect of the whole matter."

The fictional Judas College itself is a caricature of Oxford tradition in its most self-satisfied form. The description of the fifteenth-century founder, the statute requiring thirty pieces of silver to be distributed annually during Passion Week, the use of the college as a royal refuge by both Charles I and James II —all this is related in the pseudo-authoritative tone of a tourist handbook. A scene in the dining hall of Judas illustrates the ease with which scholarship in a great university reverts to pedantry. The Warden designates the Junior Fellow, Mr. Pedby, to read the Latin grace before dinner. Though internationally famous as a mathematician, Pedby is weak in Classics, and the result is disaster:

> The false quantities he made were so excruciating and so many that, while the very scouts exchanged glances, the dons at the high table lost all command of their features and made horrible noises in the effort to contain themselves. . . . Summers and winters would come and go, old faces would vanish, giving place to new, but the story of Pedby's grace would be told always. Here was a tradition that generations of dons yet unborn would cherish and chuckle over. (XXI, 308)

The undergraduates had their parallel formalities. The Junta, a club to which the Duke of Dorset belonged, was so exclusive that for a time the Duke was the only member, and he was repeatedly compelled to blackball his own suggestions for new members. The condescension with which the Duke's guest, the American Rhodes Scholar Mr. Abimilech V. Oover of Trinity College, is received, would have crushed nearly anyone except Mr. Oover. When tradition is broken by drinking the second toast to Zuleika instead of to the jilted eighteenth-century sweetheart of Junta's founder, no one objects, since in theory no member of Junta can be presumed to do wrong.

These targets of Beerbohm's satire—the New Woman, romantic love, the formalities of Oxford tradition—all suggest rather obvious, even rigid responses. They are prevented from banality by Beerbohm's structural ingenuity in developing the story and, of course, by style. The use of the minor character Noaks illustrates Beerbohm's resourcefulness. Noaks, a plebeian, a plodding scholar, has rooms above those of the Duke at Mrs. Batch's lodgings. Noaks enters the story moments after the Duke rides by and first beholds Zuleika. Zuleika notices Noaks and learns that he, too, is a student at Judas. Will he be dining at the Warden's that evening, along with the Duke? Certainly not, says the Warden. The next morning it is to Noaks that the Duke confides his love for Zuleika, only to discover that Noaks himself has fallen in love with the enchantress. It is Noaks, by snarling "And of course she's in love with you," who first raises in the Duke's mind the question of whether his love is returned. Zuleika's arrival at the Duke's rooms a little later provides the stunning negative to that question.

Noaks reappears where we should least expect to find him, at the end of the novel. Noaks, too, had intended to die for Zuleika; but, of all the undergraduates, he alone was too cowardly. That evening Zuleika strolls into the street where the Duke (and Noaks) lodged. When she sees Noaks in the window, she acclaims him as the one man in all the world masterful enough to deserve her love. But Noaks's cowardice is revealed by Katie Batch, the landlady's daughter. Katie is delighted to mock Zuleika, for Katie herself had been devoted to the Duke and jealously regarded Zuleika as a rival. Moreover, Katie had but a few minutes before Zuleika's arrival become engaged to Noaks. Katie now listens as Noaks vows to Zuleika that he did indeed love her and that only an accident had prevented him from throwing himself in the river with the other students. When Katie scornfully exposes his lie and his cowardice, poor Noaks kills himself before Zuleika's eyes by jumping into the street below. The previous climax of mass suicide is topped. The death of Noaks is an individual act. And, unlike the Duke, whose death is fated, Noaks dies by an act of free will.

Aside from the complexity of this interwoven action, a feature of the structure is the use of portents and preternatural events. In part, this is parody of classical story and medieval romance; in part, it is a suitable extension of Zuleika herself, who is by profession a conjurer, and by temperament an enchantress. At the very arrival of Zuleika, the statues of the Roman emperors on the Sheldonian Theatre feel apprehension, and beads of perspiration glisten on their stony brows. Later, as Zuleika walks by with the Duke, the emperors exchange glances, powerless to ward off the catastrophe they foresee. They are similarly apprehensive about Katie, and dubious about her engagement to Noaks. Individually, these portents might be dismissed as mere fanciful decoration. Taken together, they create a necessary atmosphere for two central uses of the preternatural: the pearls which, by changing color, symbolize the changing relationship between the Duke and Zuleika, and the owls whose warning announces the Duke's fate.

There are four pearls, Zuleika's two earrings and the Duke's two shirt studs. Separately or together, they are mentioned nearly thirty times. At the Warden's dinner party, the Duke notices that one of Zuleika's earrings is pink; the other, black. When he later sees that his own shirt studs have turned to pink and black, he realizes the strength of his attraction to Zuleika. As the story proceeds, the color of the pearls changes with the mood of the love affair: white for true love, pink and black for dangerous attraction. Emphasis of the pearls makes possible two final gestures of thwarted love. Before his death, the Duke gives Zuleika's earrings to Katie, who is thus able to taunt Zuleika with them as she stands in the street, talking to Noaks. Zuleika, in turn, gives the Duke's shirt studs to her maid.

The two owls who traditionally announce the approaching death of the Dukes of Dorset are first explained when the young Duke describes to Zuleika his titles and estates. Later, Zuleika recalls the owls as she hears the Duke play Chopin's "Marche Funèbre" at the concert, and again as the Duke takes her home. The owls are thus familiarly ominous when the telegram comes from the ducal estate. The fatality of their appearance cancels the Duke's clever plan for revenge on Zuleika; it also cancels her plea for forgiveness and a return to mutual love.

Another structural feature of the novel is the interlude (Chapters XI, XII, and XIII) in which the narrator describes himself as servant of Clio, muse of history, with special powers to transcend ordinary human perception. Chapter X concludes with the episode of Zuleika's emptying her water jug on the Duke's upturned face. Zuleika's "Now I've done it" suggests her sense of finality. The Duke can do nothing but go away, and the story can hardly proceed until morning. Even so, a change of pace and perspective is required before it does. Hence the interlude, in which epic conventions are adapted to the purpose. Clio, dissatisfied with her historians, now spends most of her time reading novels. At length, she persuades Zeus to extend to her narrator the "invisibility, inevitability, and psychic penetration" long enjoyed by novelists. As a result, the narrator can follow the Duke to his rooms after Zuleika's humiliating prank, and also look in on other students composing their wills and otherwise preparing themselves for the great romantic gesture the following day. With the coming of dawn, the narrator observes the Duke at his window. He has decided that the courageous thing to do is to renounce his vow and to save not only himself but all Oxford. With a sense of release, "He threw wide his arms in welcome of the great adorable day . . ." (XIII, 204).

Thus the interlude has advanced the action by creating a new mood in which it can continue. Rooted in classical tradition, the interlude employs parody, the beauty of Oxford at night, and the deep human impulse to live rather than die. While in his new mood, the Duke receives the telegram informing him that the owls have hooted. Despite his new resolve, his death is fated.

The elements of which *Zuleika Dobson* is composed—the New Woman, the life of privilege, Oxford tradition, Zuleika's association with London music halls, the echoes of classic legend—are brought together with extraordinary structural skill. Without an even more skillful style, however, the book could not succeed. The style is a blend of wit and beauty so subtle that shifts in tone occur before they can be distinguished. Description is filled with evocative echoes, and dialogue moves easily from the colloquial to the grandiloquent. If it is asked why Beerbohm never wrote another novel, there is only this reply: he had done the satiric fantasy as well as it could be done; and he never found another kind of story that he wished to develop into a novel.[4]

II A Christmas Garland *(1912)*

Encouraged by the success of *Zuleika Dobson*, Beerbohm selected eight of his early parodies, wrote nine new ones, and published the group under a title he had used in *The Saturday Review* in 1896. Of the seventeen parodies in *A Christmas Garland* only seven or eight deal with authors still prominent enough to make the point immediately enjoyable, as it should be: Henry James, Rudyard Kipling, H. G. Wells, Thomas Hardy, Joseph Conrad, G. B. Shaw, George Meredith, and perhaps George Moore.

Of these the first, "The Mote in the Middle Distance," is the most famous and is probably the best of the many parodies of James. The first sentence is an excellent illustration of Beerbohm's method as parodist:

> It was with the sense of a, for him, very memorable something that he peered now into the immediate future, and tried, not without compunction, to take the period up where he had, prospectively, left it.[5]

The obtrusive qualifiers, "for him," "not without compunction," and "prospectively" hit off James's curious combination of precision and tentative suggestion. The abstract words—"a very memorable something"—point up the frequent vagueness of statement. The two-faced negative "not without" registers the straining for nuance. Farther on, the parody picks up such mannerisms as the colloquial phrase set off in quotation marks ("ring off"); the italics and conspicuous adverb ("They so indubitably *are,* you know!"); and the gallicism "of an obsessiveness." Such peculiarities of James's phrasing are held together by a bogus sense of continuity that gives only the illusion of sensible discussion. It is agreeable to know that James himself enjoyed this parody.

The method of the other parodies is similar. That of Kipling begins: "I had spent Christmas Eve at the Club listening to a grand pow-wow between certain of the choicer sons of Adam" (13). At once we are reminded of Kipling's slangy colloquialism —"grand pow-wow"—and his fondness for elegant variation— "choicer sons of Adam." In "Perkins and Mankind" Beerbohm parodies Wells's penchant for juxtaposing a belligerent commoner and members of the aristocracy. In "A Sequelula to *The Dynasts*" Beerbohm opens his version of the "Fore Scene" of the epic-drama with this question by the Spirit of the Pities: "Yonder, that swarm of things insectual / Wheeling Nowhither in Particular— / What is it?" (61). "Insectual" suggests Hardy's fondness for invented and sometimes incongruous word forms. "Nowhither in Particular" typifies his inadvertent combination of the grandiloquent and the commonplace.

In "The Feast," Joseph Conrad's projection of human emotion into nature is caught in the second paragraph: "The roofs of congested trees, writhing in some kind of agony private and eternal, made tenebrous and shifty silhouettes in the sky. . . ." Conrad's awkward lapses in English idiom appear in such expressions as "The hut in which slept the white man" and "That is they." Shaw in "A Straight Talk" presents a preface to a Christmas play on Saint George. Admitting that he stole the play from the mummers in Hardy's *The Return of the Native,* Shaw insists that he has stiffened the story with "civistic conscience." It is this "civistic conscience that makes a man of me and (incidentally) makes this play a masterpiece."

In "Euphemia Clashthought," the flashy effusiveness of Meredith appears in the description of Euphemia: "She had breadth. Heels that spread ample curves over the ground she stood on, and hands that might floor you with a clench of them, were hers. Grey eyes that looked out lucid and fearless under swelling temples that were lost in a ruffling copse of hair. . . . One saw that she was a woman. She inspired deference."[6]

Other parodies in the volume are directed at the overquiet introspection of A. C. Benson, the bumptious paradoxes of G. K. Chesterton, the effrontery of Frank Harris, and academic notions of Shakespeare; at Galsworthy's sentimentality, G. B. Street's discursiveness, Hilaire Belloc's aggressive Catholicism, Maurice Hewlett's romantic medievalism, and George Moore's egotism.

One of the best parodies, "A Recollection" by Edmund Gosse, is likely to be missed because Gosse, though a leading critic from 1890 until his death in 1928, is little known to a younger generation. Gosse is represented as bringing together in Venice in 1878 Robert Browning and Henrik Ibsen. At the luncheon he arranged for the two great men, Gosse is embarrassed to discover that neither man has ever heard of the other. Browning, in deference to Ibsen, speaks Italian; but Ibsen speaks only Norwegian, which Gosse is forced to translate as tactfully as he can. On no subject do Browning and Ibsen agree. Ibsen, ignorant of Mrs. Browning's accomplishments, even insists that no woman can write good poetry. Gosse concludes gravely by recording that, though Browning did later say that Ibsen was "a capital fellow," he did not qualify the phrase; and Ibsen did not again seek Browning's company.

The skill and point of the individual parodies and the versatility in the group of seventeen make *A Christmas Garland* almost unique in the history of parody. The volume was no sudden growth, however, but the result of twenty years of experiment. Beerbohm's first recorded publication, "Carmen Becceriense" (1890), is a parody of academic editing of classical texts. "A Peep Into the Past," the long unpublished parody of Wilde, was probably written in 1894. The early magazine essays drop easily into the tone of parody, and Beerbohm as a dramatic critic frequently found parody a quick and lively way to make his point. His projected preface to Shaw's *The Devil's Disciple* has been mentioned in a previous chapter. An article on stage love scenes proceeds by parody, and a derogatory comment on *John Chilcote, M.P.* is formulated as a diagnosis by Sherlock Holmes.[7] In the collected essays parody is a common means of incidental wit, and, as has been shown, parody is a major element in *Zuleika Dobson*.

Though parody was never far from the mind of Beerbohm, his formal parodies cluster for some reason in three widely separated years. In 1896, he published a series of seven in the Christmas Supplement of *The Saturday Review*; in December, 1906, he published eight more in the *Review*; in 1912, eight old ones and nine new ones made up *A Christmas Garland.* The Meredith parody of 1896 was revised from "The Victory of Aphasia Gibberish" to the subtler "Euphemia Clashthought." The other six early parodies of Marie Corelli, Richard Le Gallienne, H. G. Wells, Ian MacLaren, Alice Meynell, and Beerbohm himself were never reprinted by the author. The 1906 series included seven of the best later collected in *A Christmas Garland,* those of James, Kipling, Wells, Chesterton, Shaw, Hewlett, and George Moore. One of John Davidson, the poet, has not been reprinted.[8] The new parodies for the 1912 volume are those of Benson, Hardy, Harris, Bennett, Galsworthy, G. B. Street, Conrad, Gosse, and Belloc. We might suppose that parody would be a form of writing congenial to Beerbohm's retirement, but after 1912 he wrote only three additional ones.

In 1915, having heard that Henry James was to receive the

Order of Merit, Beerbohm wrote an extremely witty account of the court official—"poor decent Stamfordham"—who proposed his name to the sovereign. This essay, "The Guerdon," is preferred by some to the more familiar "The Mote in the Middle Distance." Anticipating the royal question as to why the guerdon should be bestowed on Henry James, Stamfordham thinks he can only reply "Oh, well, sir, he *is*, you know—and with all submission, hang it, just *isn't* he though?—of an eminence!" When James died only a few weeks later, Beerbohm thought publication of this piece would be in poor taste, but he showed the sketch to some friends. A copy found its way to America, and it was privately printed in 1925. Beerbohm was annoyed, but he concluded that he could now properly include "The Guerdon" in his next volume, *A Variety of Things* (1928).

Another later parody is that of Maurice Baring, a versatile writer and diplomat. "All Roads," published in *John o'London's Weekly* in 1939, represents a young Englishman meeting a femme fatale at a diplomatic reception in Rome; and this parody was added to a 1950 edition of *A Christmas Garland*. "Kolniyatsch," written in 1913 and included in *And Even Now* (1920), is a parody of the current enthusiastic articles about Russian writers. Now that Luntic Kolniyatsch is dead, the narrator rushes to scrawl his name on the tombstone. Kolniyatsch, born in 1886, was "the last of a long line of ragpickers"; he became an alcoholic at nine and killed his grandmother at eighteen. Both in prose and verse, "He compasses a rhythm which is the very rhythm of life itself." For the knowing, "Kolniyatsch" readily translates to "Colney Hatch," the name of an asylum for the insane near London. "Luntic" is, therefore, a shortened form of "lunatic."

III Seven Men *(1919)*

Next to *Zuleika Dobson*, Beerbohm's most sustained creation is the collection of five narrative sketches entitled *Seven Men*. Beerbohm is involved in all of them, and one sketch concerns two men; hence the title. Though the five narratives were separately published over a period of five years and were collected only as an afterthought, a kind of unity is achieved through playful improbability and an indulgently reminiscent tone. The juxtaposition of actual people with fictional characters reduces the implausibility of events. Though not the first to appear in print, "Enoch Soames" is surely the right choice to open the volume. The sketch begins with praise of Mr. Holbrook Jackson's book on the 1890's (published in 1913)—praise, but disappointment, too, because the name of Enoch Soames is not even in the index. Then follows a seemingly factual account of Beerbohm's three meetings with Soames. The first was in the domino room of the Café Royal, in the company of Will Rothenstein. Soames, "a stooping, shambling person," stops and reminds Rothenstein of their previous meeting in Paris. Beerbohm learns that Soames is the author of a book of essays called *Negations*; but, after buying a copy, Beerbohm is never able to determine what it is about. At a second meeting, Soames reports that his book of poems, *Fungoids*, has sold only three copies.

At the third meeting, in a little Soho restaurant, Soames complains of his failure to achieve reputation during his own life, but he feels sure that posterity will recognize his genius. At this point, a stranger, who introduces himself as the Devil, offers, in return for the soul of Soames, to allow him to visit the British Museum in 1997. Soames, who then vanishes, returns much cast down, in time for dinner. In the great reading room he found no reference to his work. Even that great authority on the 1890's, T. K. Nupton, writing in the new phonetic English, mentions Soames only as an imaginary character in "a sumwot labud sattire" by Max Beerbohm. When the Devil promptly arrives to enforce his bargain, Soames, as he is carried off, implores: "Try, *try*, to make them know that I did exist!" Thus Soames stands for the man in the 1890's who only imagined that he had talent, a type readily found in any generation. Treated in 1897, the subject would have invited sharp satire; seen through a haze of reminiscence, Soames is touched with the pathos of all human striving.

Next to "Enoch Soames," the story of "Savonarola Brown" is most interesting. Beerbohm states that he had known Brown at school; and, while writing dramatic criticism for *The Saturday Review*, he frequently saw him at the theater. Brown, now passionately anxious to write a play about Savonarola, seeks Beerbohm's advice. The two men argue about the need for probability in a play. "In actual life it isn't so," said Brown. "What is there to prevent a motor-omnibus from knocking me down and killing me at this very moment?" Brown's argument was immediately substantiated, for a motor-omnibus did knock him down and kill him. Beerbohm, left with the incomplete play, feels duty-bound to publish it. It abounds in striking situations, and, says Beerbohm, "I have searched it vainly for one line that does not scan."[9]

The play which concludes the sketch is a wild parody of nineteenth-century imitators of Elizabethan drama. The fifteenth-century Savonarola is juxtaposed to the thirteenth-century Dante and Saint Francis, and to other famous Italians of assorted centuries. Savonarola is involved in a poison plot with Lucrezia Borgia. As Brown left it, the manuscript broke off with Savonarola and Lucrezia escaping from prison. Beerbohm has supplied a fifth act in which, trapped by Machiavelli, they die together by eating deadly nightshade. The action is thus a brilliant illustration of Brown's doctrine that probability should be ignored by playwrights. The verse of the play is appropriate to the action. One song begins: "When pears hang green on the garden wall/ With a nid, and a nod, and a niddy-niddy-o."

Although the other three stories show similar ingenuity, they have less intrinsic interest. "Hilary Maltby and Stephen Braxton" is about two rival novelists. Maltby, the sensitive man, is so affected by the real and imagined jibes of Braxton that he leaves England. Years later in Italy, a chance meeting with Beerbohm leads him to explain his disappearance. "James Pethel" tells of an extremely lucky gambler whose life is a succession of adventures that terrify his wife and daughter. Pethel's death, of a heart attack, prompts the telling of his story. The best feature of this sketch is the evocation of the August holidays in Dieppe that were so important to Beerbohm from 1897 to 1907. "A. V. Laider" records the strange story of an acquaintance who may—or may not—be telling the truth about a horrible train accident that fulfilled a premonition of fate, but left the narrator with a feeling of guilt about the death of friends whose death he foresaw but could not prevent.

In 1927 Beerbohm published "Not That I Would Boast," a sketch similar to those in *Seven Men*. First collected in *A Variety of Things* (1928), and eventually added to a new edition of the older book, *Seven Men and Two Others* (1950), the sketch was retitled "Felix Argallo and Walter Ledgett," to conform to its new context. In it Ledgett is an aspiring author, slighted by such great figures as Stevenson and Meredith. Beerbohm intercedes with Argallo, a successful author, to write a series of letters with admiring references to Ledgett. After Argallo's suicide these letters are published, much to the bewilderment of poor Ledgett. Beerbohm then persuades Ledgett that he has merely forgotten the many occasions on which he and Argallo were so congenial together. Once persuaded, Ledgett is able to enjoy the greatly improved literary reputation which the bogus letters have secured for him.

Another sketch included in *A Variety of Things* might well have been included in *Seven Men.* "T. Fenning Dodworth" is a satiric portrait of the man about town who knows everyone and carries himself with great assurance, yet never does anything to justify the good opinion he basks in. Having failed at law, and failed seven times to win a seat in Parliament, Dodworth took to writing articles for the reviews. It was he who invented the form of title exemplified in "The Home Rule Peril—And After." Installed as editor of a flourishing paper, Dodworth presides over its failure; but, as a reward, he is given a testimonial dinner. Characteristically, Dodworth adapted himself to the changes of the war and the postwar years. Dodworth, Beerbohm concludes, "will die game, and his last words will be 'And After?' "

Seven Men is a work of extraordinary skill, and those who take an interest in Beerbohm and his period will always delight in its verbal felicities and in its shrewd sense of character. Yet, like all parody, it is derivative and will win few readers by itself. *Zuleika Dobson* and the sketches in *Seven Men* suggest that Beerbohm had capacities for fiction that for reasons obscure even to himself he never fully developed.

IV *Other Fiction and Drama*

Besides *Zuleika Dobson* and *Seven Men,* Beerbohm wrote several other stories, and he made a few attempts at drama. They do not add much to his achievement, but they show a capacity for more varied experiment than might be anticipated from his more familiar works. They suggest also that he found the role of essayist, wit, and satirist not wholly satisfying.

As dramatist, Beerbohm joined the long list of dramatic critics who, knowing a great deal about the stage and having great skill with words, have yet been unable to write great or even good plays. His first attempt, the one-act dramatization of *The Happy Hypocrite* in 1900, was his most successful. Beerbohm wrote Turner that the play had been given five curtain calls at its first performance; he did not care what the reviewers might say. As a curtain-raiser for Frank Harris's *Mr. and Mrs. Daventry,* the play ran for several weeks and earned Beerbohm more than a hundred pounds. Even so, its success must have owed much to Beerbohm's personal reputation. In 1902 Beerbohm collaborated with Harris in adapting Paul Hervieu's *L'Enigme* as *Caesar's Wife.* In reviewing the play on March 8, Beerbohm pointed out some improbabilities in the action, but he did not indicate that he himself had had a part in adapting the play for the English stage. In the same year, Beerbohm and S. Murray Carson wrote a comedy, *The Fly on the Wheel.* In 1907 the idea for a play with a hero modeled on Winston Churchill looked promising, but nothing came of this.[10]

In 1913 and again in 1914 a one-act play, *A Social Success,* was produced as a curtain-raiser. The text of the play, included in *A Variety of Things,* is not impressive. Tommy Dixon, an attractive and popular young man, is caught cheating at cards by his aristocratic friends. It then turns out that he has cheated deliberately in order to escape the boredom of being a social success. The aristocratic friends like him so much, however, that they relent; they not only apologize, but invent elaborate explanations to smooth over the scandal. Tommy, it turns out, is simply too attractive to be dropped; he will have to remain a social success. The dialogue of the play is lively, the motivations are preposterous as those in Wilde's comedies, and the adaptation of Sheridan's screen scene in *The School for Scandal* is deftly brought off. Yet the effect is trivial. It is Beerbohm's fame that gives interest to his efforts in drama. They add little to his fame.

"The Dreadful Dragon of Hay Hill," a fable written during World War I, was first published in *A Variety of Things,* but it was also separately issued as a small book in the same year (1928). In terms of fantasy, the story makes ironic comments on human nature. In the London area of ancient Britain a fiery dragon suddenly appears. Thol, the boy who first saw the dragon, learns how to kill him and becomes the hero-god of the little community. The beautiful Thia becomes his bride. As a god, Thol is no longer permitted to herd his sheep, and in his idleness he and Thia quarrel. Free from danger, the villagers revert to dull routine; and the careless youths spend their time in dancing. When Thol joins their revels, Thia refuses to accompany him. In order to win her back, Thol simulates a new dragon in the cave of the old one; he spends his days gathering wood for the nightly fires that are part of the deception. The people renounce Thol, for he refuses to kill the new dragon; Thia, pitying him, joins in the deception. Eventually Thia dies, and not long afterward, Thol himself dies. When Thol's body is found and the trick is understood, the villagers blame Thia for the deception and bury Thol with honor.

References to present-day Berkeley Square, Green Park, and Soho invite readers to make such comparisons and contrasts with modern life as they can. The dragon, no doubt, is the world war; reference to the pleasure-seeking youth is a comment on the England of the 1920's; and the neglect of Thol in middle age is the fickleness of the public toward wartime heroes. The final paragraph includes one of the many comments on the vanity and weakness of human nature; for the sake of Thol and Thia, Beerbohm says: "We wish that the good they did could have been lasting. But it is not in the nature of things that anything —except the nature of things—should last. Saints and wise statesmen can do much. Their reward is in the doing of it. They are lucky if they do not live long enough to see the undoing."[11] Such comments reflect the general sadness so frequent in Beerbohm's later years.

"The Dreadful Dragon," like *The Happy Hypocrite,* will win few readers for Beerbohm. Yet for those already attuned to his stance and style, there is many a sly and characteristic touch. There is Veo the artist, unconcerned about public danger but anxious to get a good look at the dragon so he can paint it. There is Shib, the counselor who gives sage advice to Thol on how heroes should comport themselves in public. Yet as a whole, the fable does not quite succeed. Why should it be said that Thol and Thia are happier in deception than in the genuine heroism of their youth? Perhaps it is because they are isolated from society and free from its pretensions, as Max and Florence were. But deception is not superior to pretension, and the parallel with Max and Florence hardly fits. When "The Dreadful Dragon" was first published, a reviewer observed rather hopelessly that the point of the story must be that it is absurd for us to draw any moral from human conduct.[12]

In the later volumes of essays, as in the earlier ones, there are occasional essays that come close to fictional narrative. "William and Mary," for example, is a condensed novel about a young writer who makes an idyllic marriage, loses his wife in childbirth, goes to Africa as war correspondent, and is killed there. The story is told through memories called to mind by sight of the deserted house once so happily occupied by the young couple. Though the method is fictional, "William and Mary" is said to have been based on the life of a friend.[13]

One ambitious work of fiction Beerbohm began about 1913 but never finished. It was to be called *The Mirror of the Past,* a title suggested by the convex mirror he prized so highly.[14] The mirror of the fiction was to have the magical power to retain previous images, so that it preserved a visual record of the meetings reflected in it. For this project Beerbohm wrote the sketches of George Moore, the Irish novelist, and Nat Goodwin, the American actor, later used in radio broadcasts and included in the posthumous edition of *Mainly on the Air.* These pieces proceed in informal narrative, with reminiscences that blend dialogue and scene. George Moore is represented as talking with Edmund Gosse about *Don Quixote.* When Gosse suggests that Sancho Panza is mad from the outset of the story, Moore replies: "I had not thought of that. [*Thinks of it, with growing pleasure in the idea.*] That is a good i-de-a, Gosse. I do not say that it is a true i-de-a. But an i-de-a is an i-de-a whether it be . . . [*His voice drifts into silence.*] . . ." (83).

Many other passages might be cited to show how fictional was the method of Beerbohm's mind. When we say that his style is "lively," that is what we mean. An idea, or a mental trait of an individual, is picked up and projected as gesture or tone of voice. This capability, to judge from recorded samples, was the fascination of Beerbohm's talk. Why so fictional a mind should have produced only one novel and a handful of sketches is puzzling—but not so puzzling, perhaps, as the high and individual quality of his best work.

V *Later Essays*

And Even Now (1920) is Beerbohm's finest collection of essays. All twenty were written during the years of retirement, most of them between 1918 and 1920. Even the journalistic variations on easy themes are more deliberate and more definitive than similar pieces in earlier collections. "How Shall I Word It?" satirizes a "complete letter writer" by giving models of truthful indignation instead of the stilted letters in the self-help book. The dullness of going for a walk with an insistent friend, the desirability of wrapping up all public statues ("A Mobled King"), the ugliness of old railway cars clustered on a hillside for dwellings ("Homes Unblest") are other congenial but not highly original topics.

"Something Defeasible" describes a boy's sand castle destroyed by the tide in such a way as to suggest the threat in Labour's projected reforms. "Servants"—Beerbohm was afraid of them—is a thoughtful speculation about the unnatural relation between masters and servants; it closes with the hope that domestic service will somehow disappear altogether. "On Speaking French" comes to a witty climax in an anecdote of confusion. Like other Englishmen. Beerbohm has long taken refuge in the innocuous phrase, "C'est vrai." When a French lady asks who is the most popular French novelist in England, he inadvertently replies "C'est vrai." The lady is immediately mystified by his reference to a French novelist "Sevré" of whom she has never heard.

Two essays are more than incidentally autobiographical. "A Relic" recalls, or invents, an account of Beerbohm's boyish attempt to write a story in the manner of Maupassant. Confident that he "knew life," since he had learned about it from Maupassant's stories, he tried to develop a story from a glimpse of a quarrel between a man and a woman in a French cafe. Alas! Plausible events to develop the story would not suggest themselves, and only a single atmospheric sentence was actually composed: "Down below, the sea rustled to and fro over the shingle."

In "Hosts and Guests," Beerbohm divides people into the two classes of the title, and shrewdly analyzes his own uneasiness as host and his habitual pleasure in being a guest. This simple contrast is embellished by unexpected illustrations drawn from *Macbeth*, the Borgias, *The Pickwick Papers*, and the habitually ungrateful Dante.

The essays most likely to be reread, however, are the directly literary ones. Of these "No. 2 The Pines," a droll but affectionate account of Beerbohm's acquaintance with Swinburne, is the most distinguished, and the hardest to parallel in the comments of other writers on literary figures. Beerbohm begins by emphasizing the remoteness of Swinburne in 1899, when they first met. Swinburne, in public imagination, was still the rhapsodist of 1865 and 1866 when he had published *Atalanta in Calydon* and *Poems and Ballads.* Because of his illness, deafness, and generally impractical nature, Swinburne had for twenty years lived in a kind of protective custody with Theodore Watts-Dunton, a minor poet and novelist who took friendly notice of Beerbohm's early writings. Beerbohm gladly, but with some nervousness, accepted an invitation to lunch. In the hallway he was aware of "an odd august past" in the Rossetti drawings on the walls.

When Swinburne entered the dining room, his formal bow, his tiny fluttering hands, and his high cooing voice made contradictory impressions. On a later visit, Beerbohm was embarrassed when Swinburne showed him his great library, containing treasure after treasure that Beerbohm, in his ignorance, had never heard of. Watts-Dunton's care of Swinburne had its comic side; but, as acquaintance grew, Beerbohm came to respect the relationship. The essay concludes by describing a possible meeting in Elysium, in which Watts-Dunton is reunited with Rossetti and Swinburne, with Dante and the great Italian patriot Mazzini standing by.

The fancy of this incidental touch becomes a structural element in developing an interpretation of a passage in Boswell's *Johnson*. The unimpressive title, "A Clergyman," may conceal for some readers one of Beerbohm's most skillful essays. He describes the clergyman thus: "Fragmentary, pale, momentary; almost nothing; glimpsed and gone; as it were, a faint human hand thrust up, never to reappear, from beneath the rolling waters of Time, he forever haunts my memory and solicits my weak imagination. Nothing is told of him but that once, abruptly, he asked a question, and received an answer."[15]

The question, Beerbohm explains, was asked on April 7, 1778, at the home of the Thrales, whom Johnson and Boswell often visited. On this occasion, Boswell questioned the great doctor about the best writers of sermons. Atterbury, Tillotson, Seed,

Jortin, Sherlock, Smalridge, and Ogden were approved by Dr. Johnson with those nice distinctions of compliment of which he was master. Then said Boswell:

What I want to know is, what sermons afford the best specimen of English pulpit eloquence.
Johnson: We have no sermons addressed to the passions, that are good for anything; if you mean that kind of eloquence.
A Clergyman, whose name I do not recollect: Were not Dodd's sermons addressed to the passions?
Johnson: They were nothing, Sir, be they addressed to what they may. (234)

"The suddenness of it!" says Beerbohm. "Bang!—and the rabbit that had popped from its burrow was no more." Beerbohm then speculates about this mysterious clergyman. Who was he? Why had Boswell not mentioned him earlier? Why did he not remember his name? He must have been a shy young man, probably the curate from the nearby church. The question, carefully inspected, is one which must have been uttered in a high thin voice that grated on the ears of the slightly deaf Dr. Johnson: "Were not Dodd's sermons addressed to the passions?" Hopeful of praise for his suggestion, the young clergyman probably never recovered from Johnson's rebuff: "He sank into a rapid decline. Before the next blossoming of Thrale Hall's almond trees he was no more. I like to think that he died forgiving Dr. Johnson" (241).

One of the slyest touches in this essay is a parody of Johnson's remarks on sermon writers, in which Beerbohm substitutes the names of contemporary novelists. In such a piece as "A Clergyman" the full possibility of the essay is realized. There is sharp recollection, there is discovery, there is satiric juxtaposition. Pathos is checked by a laugh at human folly, and the laugh is checked before it sours into cynicism.

"Books within Books" is another remarkable illustration of Beerbohm's acute memory and of his wide reading. In a few pages he mentions some twenty titles of books said to have been written by characters in novels, titles that tantalize because the volumes are imaginary and unattainable. How agreeable it would be to read *Walter Lorraine,* the early novel by Thackeray's Arthur Pendennis. Henry James provides several titles: there is

Shadowmere by Henry St. George in "The Lesson of the Master," and Ray Limbert's *The Major Key* in "The Next Time." Above all, Beerbohm would like to read Austin Feverel's *The Pilgrim's Scrip*, so often quoted in Meredith's *The Ordeal of Richard Feverel.*

"Quia Imperfectum" ("Because Imperfect") begins with a similar meditation on the charm of unfinished works, such as Coleridge's "Kubla Khan" and Dickens's *The Mystery of Edwin Drood.* This reverie leads to an analysis of Goethe based on a description of the unfinished portrait by Wilhelm Tischbein. Why was it left unfinished? Tischbein was a painter of some reputation in the romantic historical style of the eighteenth century. The portrait was begun in Italy, and for some time poet and artist were constantly together. Reading between the lines of Goethe's *Travels in Italy* and other sources, Beerbohm infers that Tischbein became bored with the great man. What happened to the unfinished portrait remains a mystery, but Beerbohm covets it for his projected museum of incomplete masterpieces.

The dozen items in *A Variety of Things* (1928) have all been separately discussed under other topics. As the title suggests, the volume pretended no unity, such as the earlier volumes had indirectly achieved. *A Variety of Things* was originally published as the tenth and last volume of the collected edition (1922-28), and it was thus a kind of appendix to the set. Offered separately for sale, it served a similar purpose for readers already familiar with the author.

In its original edition, *Mainly on the Air* (1946) was a slender volume of only a hundred and thirty pages. Even so, it was filled out by reprinting from *A Variety of Things* "T. Fenning Dodworth" and the journalistic "A Note on the Einstein Theory." Aside from the six radio talks, discussed in an earlier chapter, only three essays were new. "From Bloomsbury to Bayswater" (1940), already discussed, contrasts Bloomsbury unfavorably with the Bayswater region in London where Beerbohm lived as a young man. "Top Hat" (1940) recalls the omnipresence of top hats in the England of his youth, when even crossing sweepers wore them. In "Fenestralia" (1944), which is similarly reminiscent, Beerbohm recalls scenes from Paris, London, and Italy, which are framed for him by the windows he looked out. Especially memorable is a momentary sight of Degas in Paris. With these three late reminiscences was grouped "Old Carthusian Memories" from a 1920 issue of the school magazine.

To a posthumous edition of *Mainly on the Air* (1957) Beerbohm's Rede lecture on Lytton Strachey was added. When he delivered the lecture at Cambridge in 1943, Beerbohm spoke of himself as an old man of seventy. The discussion of Strachey, however, avoids garrulity; and the evaluation of Strachey is informed and intellectually alive. Beerbohm begins by describing his first view of Strachey at the Savile Club in 1912. Strachey, then thirty-two, was little known as yet, but he was conspicuous in the quiet club with his velveteen jacket, soft shirt, and dark red tie. Later, Beerbohm met Strachey several times; and, beginning with the publication of *Eminent Victorians* (1918), he followed his work with great admiration.

Beerbohm saw Strachey's work sympathetically, as an extension of the witty attack on the Victorianism of his own youth. The great popularity of Strachey in the 1920's was followed by reaction after his death in 1932. When Beerbohm delivered his lecture in 1943, he conceded that Strachey had too little sympathy for strength of character, and he thus undervalued people like Dr. Thomas Arnold, Florence Nightingale, and Queen Victoria herself. Strachey's greatness was in his sense of form and in his superb narrative skill. He was an uncommon man, such as may be greatly valued when the century of the common man has passed away. The argument is developed with easy allusions to the many historical figures treated by Strachey, and by illuminating references to other writers as diverse as Boswell, Macaulay, Pater, Stevenson, Herbert Spencer, and D. H. Lawrence. Those who heard the lecture, like those who heard the radio talks, remarked on the beauty of diction in Beerbohm's spoken words.

VI *Uncollected Works*

Between 1910 and 1956 Beerbohm published only about sixty magazine articles, hardly more than one a year, in some twenty journals, including the American *Atlantic Monthly, Century, Harper's Weekly, Harper's Monthly,* and *Living Age*. The best of these articles Beerbohm himself collected, but a few others justify brief mention. An essay written for the library of the

Queen's Doll House celebrates gracefully the charm of smallness. The "Memorial Address" for Beerbohm's old friend Sir William Rothenstein, though brief, is a model for such occasions. "When I Was Nineteen," a reminiscent account of Beerbohm's early caricatures in *The Strand* (1893), belongs with the other autobiographical sketches.

Several of the letters to the editor make comments of more than passing interest: a tribute to his old friend Sir Edward Marsh, patron of literature and secretary to Winston Churchill; a proposal for a crossword puzzle that would have *no* solution; a comment on Duse; and a letter expressing delight in the illustrated books of James and Muirhead Bone.

There is also a late review (1949) of a reissue of Henry James's *A Little Tour in France* (first published in 1882). *Max in Verse* (1963) printed for the first time a dialect sonnet to Henry James, supposedly written by Miss Peploe, a dressmaker in Rye who worshiped the Master from afar. Among the notes to new editions of Beerbohm's own books and to those of his friends is many a memorable sentence. When S. C. Roberts published *Zuleika in Cambridge* in 1941, this comment from Beerbohm appeared on the cover: "I had often wondered what happened when Zuleika went to Cambridge, and now I *know,* beyond any shadow of a doubt."

Fragmentary and unpretentious as many of the uncollected works are, there is something characteristic about them. The easy grace is a by-product of disciplined attention. The wit has its source in habitual reflection on the incongruities of life. The genial manner is restrained, partly from a consideration of others, partly from a defensive sense of privacy. Lacking massive power, Beerbohm acquired the art of suggesting reserves of mind and heart that in their own degree communicate to readers that heightened awareness which we call interest.

CHAPTER 6

The Caricatures

NO DISCUSSION of Beerbohm as a writer can ignore his caricatures. Many of his most memorable drawings are of literary men such as Wilde, Kipling, and Shaw. The writer who skeptically analyzed Shaw's plays and the artist who drew Shaw standing on his head were the same man. Moreover, the artist pointed up the effect of his drawing by putting himself in it and adding these words: "Mild surprise of one who, revisiting England after long absence, finds that the dear fellow has not moved."[1] Beerbohm condemned the illustration of literary texts, and his early drawings make their point without captions. By 1900, however, the typical Beerbohm caricature combines visual and verbal effect.

Beerbohm's principal comments on caricature appear in two early essays. "A. B."[2] is a tribute to Arthur Bryan, a prolific draughtsman of the 1890's. Beerbohm calculates that he sees each year in such now-forgotten magazines as *Judy* and *Moonshine* some eleven hundred new drawings by Bryan. The spontaneity and skill of the work are what pleases Beerbohm, not its perfection. In the course of the essay praise is also given to the drawings of Phil May, especially known for his good-natured sketches of slum children; to Leslie Ward, the "Spy" whose mildly satirical portraits appeared weekly in *Vanity Fair*; and to Leonard Raven-Hill, who had provided a brief introduction to Beerbohm's first volume of drawings.

A few years later in "The Spirit of Caricature,"[3] Beerbohm asked the question: "Why is true caricature so rare and unpopular in England?" The true spirit of caricature, he then says, was brought from Italy by Carlo Pellegrini, the "Ape" of *Vanity Fair* and the predecessor and tutor of Leslie Ward. English criticism caused Pellegrini's work to decline in quality. Thinking of the plight of caricature in England, Beerbohm invents a dream in which he is summoned to be the professor in a vast School of National Caricature. Happily, he awoke before he gave his inaugural lecture, but the latter part of the essay explains what he would like to have said. He would have denied that caricatures are motivated by irreverence or cruelty, and that they are unlike their subjects. The exaggeration of caricature is necessary, but it is largely unconscious; it is based on study, and it must be free from the restraining presence of the model. Caricature, he says, "is a form of wit, and nothing so ruthlessly chokes laughter as the suspicion of labour."

In these two essays there is no very solid basis for a theory of caricature. The essay on Bryan praises him for his ability to draw theatrical scenes while watching the play; the presence of the models did not "restrain" Bryan. When Beerbohm denies that caricatures are motivated by irreverence or cruelty, we think of his many drawings of Kipling and of Edward VII. Cruelty is perhaps too strong a word for the emphatic vulgarity attributed to Kipling and the beak-nosed grossness of Edward, but at least there is some malice. As we have noted, Beerbohm later admitted a feeling of guilt for his treatment of Kipling, and he explained his discontinuance of caricature after 1925 by saying: "It's a young man's hobby—you get kinder as you get older."[4] The idea that Beerbohm's conception of caricature was wholly esthetic is hardly tenable. He used caricature to mock what he thought ridiculous, irrational, or wrong; sometimes he mocked with affection, sometimes with that touch of malice so frequent in wit of all kinds.

Besides these inconsistencies, it is strange that Beerbohm ignored the vigorous English tradition of caricature which flourished long before Pelligrini. There is no reference to William Hogarth (1697–1764), James Gillray (1757–1815), and Thomas Rowlandson (1756–1827). Hogarth's serious paintings hardly earned him the fame and reward brought by such caricatures as "A Harlot's Progress," "A Rake's Progress," "Marriage à la Mode," and "Election Series." Gillray was a political caricaturist whose savage lampoons were solicited by both Whigs and Tories. Rowlandson was perhaps more of a comic illustrator than a caricaturist, but his drawings for more than a hundred volumes —such as the novels of Fielding, Smollett, and Sterne—made collectors' items.[5]

These artists, it is true, favored a complexity very different from Beerbohm's customary simplicity. Rowlandson's "Vauxhall

Gardens," for example, shows fifty men and women gathered under the trees, as they listen to a lady who sings from a formally decorated balcony. Many in the crowd are gaunt or fat to the point of ugliness as they flirt and ogle, eat and applaud. Yet there is in the composition a grace that is enhanced by the soft tints of the blue sky, green trees, and varied costumes. It is surprising that Beerbohm, with his great fondness for the eighteenth century, never alludes to Rowlandson, Gillray, Hogarth, and their many imitators.

The mid-nineteenth century, with its wealth of periodicals and illustrated books, developed its own tradition of caricature. Thackeray (1811-63) illustrated much of his own early work. Hablôt K. Browne (1815-82), the "Phiz" who illustrated the novels of Dickens, made comic drawings a household possession. Other popular artists were George Cruikshank (1792–1878), John Doyle (1798–1868), George du Maurier (1834–96), John Leech (1817–83), and John Tenniel (1820–1914). Leech, du Maurier, and Tenniel were especially identified with *Punch*, one of the weekly delights of Beerbohm's boyhood. Tenniel was universally known as the illustrator of *Alice in Wonderland* (1865).

Against this background, Carlo Pellegrini (1839–89) began to furnish weekly caricatures for *Vanity Fair* in 1862. Ten years later Leslie Ward became his assistant, and later his successor. Between them, "Ape" and "Spy" contributed weekly drawings from 1862 until 1907. In later years, as Beerbohm says, the element of caricature almost disappeared; but the portrait-drawings were so popular that they were reproduced in great numbers. Pellegrini and Ward not only stimulated Beerbohm in a personal way; they helped materially to create a market for his caricatures.

I *Early Drawings*

As a small child, Max amused himself by drawing; and he was pleased to find that his admired half-brother Herbert shared this pleasure. Herbert, who became an actor when Max was six, was always seeing celebrities such as Disraeli, Whistler, and Wilde; and, when at home, he sketched them for the family. Max's own favorite subjects at this time were policemen and, later, politicians. It has been mentioned that at Orme School, which he attended from nine to thirteen, Mrs. Wilkinson, wife of the master, gave Max the only drawing lessons he ever had. At Charterhouse, during the years 1885 to 1890, he continued to draw. In the school library there survives an eight-page manuscript in verse, "An Epic of Hades," illustrated by "M. B." with some thirty-four drawings, chiefly caricatures of the masters. The Minute Book of the Charterhouse Society also contains some drawings. Larger caricatures of Dr. Haig Brown, the headmaster, and of several other masters are framed and hung on the library walls. Most of these early drawings are crude scribbling, as might be expected, but there are suggestions of Beerbohm's later style.[6]

At Merton College, Max drew several of the dons. George Brodrick, the bearded Warden, was a tempting subject. A group sketch showing Brodrick and four others is said to have been drawn during an examination. According to Will Rothenstein, who met Max in 1893, the sale of such caricatures at Shrimpton's, an Oxford printshop, contributed to Max's local fame. John Lane, who had commissioned Rothenstein to draw a folio of Oxford portraits, considered publishing another series by Max, but the plan was given up.

The first Beerbohm caricatures to be published were a series of "Club Types" in *The Strand* of 1892. Many years later Beerbohm contributed to that magazine an account of how his sister had shown his caricatures to Mr. Greenough Smith, then editor.[7] Acceptance of these drawings for *The Strand* was indeed impressive recognition, for the magazine was then at the height of its popularity through the publication of the Sherlock Holmes stories. "Club Types," thirty-six drawings in all, appeared in the issues for September, November, and December. The small figures, with no captions except the names of well-known clubs, hit off social types with clever exaggeration. The Turf Clubman, with umbrella and top hat, demands a winning horse. The Guards officer needs no uniform to imply command: a huge overcoat speaks vigor, and a small head suggests a minimum of intellectual interest. The Arts Club member is appropriately spindle-legged; flowing hair and windsor tie are prominent as he leans on a small table as if about to make a speech.

In Beerbohm's account of how these drawings came to be published, he cheerfully points out some of his errors: the Savile Club was not quite so esthetically minded as his drawing suggests; the Travelers Club was actually more socially exclusive than adventurous. Such errors aside, however, the series does admirably support Beerbohm's characterization of the age: "There were in the men of those old days great dissimilarities of aspect. Every man tended to look like what he was. He followed his own line. He gave rein to his soul. He was well worth looking at." To be sure, the men of the 1890's were not quite so individual as their predecessors of the 1860's and 1870's with their "long hair, short hair, enormous beards, faces clean-shaven except for a tuft beneath the lower lip, loose clothes, tight clothes, gold-headed canes, very bad umbrellas . . . all according to taste, untrammelled taste." The Demon of Uniformity, Max concludes, slowly gathered speed in the 1890's. In 1946, the date of the article, he represented as "typical of *any* club" a nondescript and slovenly figure equipped with spectacles, cigarette, and briefcase.

Beerbohm's second appearance in *The Strand,*[8] though more than two years later, was much less notable. He illustrated Harold George's "Oxford at Home" with eight undistinguished caricatures bearing such captions as these: "Dons New School and Old School" (a venerable and robust don confronts a frail, bookish young man); "Lady Novelist's Ideal" (a broad-shouldered Adonis holding a cricket bat); "A student at Somervelle Hall" (a willowy young lady). In these drawings we find little of the skill that makes "Club Types" still interesting.

Before the Oxford article appeared, Beerbohm had left the university and had embarked upon the uncertain career of a freelance writer and caricaturist. In the penny weekly *Pick-Me-Up* he published a series of thirty-one drawings of such notable figures as Oscar Wilde, Henry Arthur Jones, Henry Irving (made to look like Aubrey Beardsley), Lord Randolph Churchill, and Arthur Balfour. Under the heading "Personal Remarks," the series ran from September 15, 1894, to April 20, 1895, and thus included the months during which Beerbohm was touring America with Beerbohm Tree. *Pick-Me-Up* featured situation cartoons, short fictional sketches, verse, some photographs, and some non-humorous line drawings. Weekly departments headed "Our Pepper Pot," "Through the Opera Glass," and "The Voice of the Lyre" indicate the popular appeal of the publication.

The series of caricatures in *Pick-Me-Up*—together with a few in *The Pall-Mall Budget,* and two in *The Savoy* (1896), along with numerous prose pieces—prepared the way for the publication of *Caricatures of Twenty-five Gentlemen* in December, 1896. On the purple-blue cloth cover of this volume a gold line drawing shows a top-hatted Max, dressed as Harlequin, grasping a pen taller than himself. The title page is ornamented by a small Beardsley drawing of Harlequin mounted on Pegasus, a design repeated in gold on the back cover. The book is dedicated "To the shade of Carlo Pellegrini," the "Ape" of *Vanity Fair.* In the preface, Leonard Raven-Hill, himself a popular cartoonist, admitted Max's defects as draughtsman: "I know he can't correctly reproduce a foot or the shadows on a face, and that his perspective is apt to be a bit primitive; but he makes up greatly for this lack of technical knowledge by a charming freedom of line." Raven-Hill added that he would not advise Max to *learn* drawing; doing so might make him self-conscious.

Of the twenty-five subjects represented in this volume, ten were political figures; the rest are chiefly literary and stage personalities. In caricaturing them, Beerbohm used three common devices: the exaggerated head; the exaggeration of thinness or heaviness of the figure; and the miniature which reduces reputation to triviality. Lord Rosebery, the Prince of Wales, Frank Harris, Rudyard Kipling, and Joseph Chamberlain are all depicted with large heads; Rosebery with flabby jowls and vacuous expression; Frank Harris with mustache jutting out above a fancy waistcoat and prominent boutonniere; Kipling, jut-jawed, mustached, and crop-haired; Chamberlain with a nose that makes grotesque angles with his lower jaw and forehead.

The opposite of such grossness is suggested by Arthur Balfour, whose tiny face perches at the top of a thin body winding upward in a reversed figure *S,* his long arm clutching a dispatch box. Whether or not one is familiar with the long career of Balfour, it is clear at a glance that he is the intellectual in politics, his ideas far removed from the beefy concerns of ordinary mortals. Lord William Nevill, in impeccable evening dress, has legs so long and thin that he seems mounted on stilts. Shaw's rather normal figure is elongated by the device of emphasizing a tiny hand holding an umbrella. The pianist Paderewski is a very small figure surmounted by a cloud of hair. Richard Le Gallienne's wispy body, decorated with a flowing windsor tie, carries the eye to a head that is a blur of horizontal lines. Aubrey Beardsley's large head, with sail-like nose, skullcap of hair, and no eyes seems to overbalance the slender body below, which is further diminished by the toy dog on a leash. There is a similar contrast between George Moore's bulbous head and his diminutive trunk, arms, and legs.

A few figures are shown in normal proportion: Arthur Wing Pinero, the dramatist; George Alexander and Herbert Beerbohm Tree, the actors; Robert Hichens, the novelist; Henry Harland, editor of *The Yellow Book;* and Henry Chaplin, the country gentleman M.P. These men are caricatured chiefly through large eyebrows, toothy smiles, or the suggestion of animated movement.

II *Max's Nineties (1958)*

A recent collection[9] brings together forty-six Beerbohm caricatures from the 1890's, nine of them from the 1896 volume, twenty-five from various magazines, and a series on Gladstone not previously reproduced. The magazine drawings increase our awareness of Beerbohm's early industry, and his alertness to public interest in such figures as the novelist Robert Hichens, the dramatic critic A. B. Walkley, and Henry James.

The series of eleven drawings on Gladstone, however, is the major interest in this volume. After a long career as leader of the Liberal party, William Ewart Gladstone died May 19, 1898. He had three times served as prime minister, and for a generation he had opposed Disraeli. Gladstone's power rested on his great eloquence and on his capacity to present himself as the personification of high moral principle. Beerbohm's series of caricatures, entitled "Mr. Gladstone Goes to Heaven," was done within a week after the death of the great man. The drawings were privately sold and were never exhibited until 1945.[10] The series makes brilliant use of captions to sharpen the point of each drawing.

The first drawing shows Gladstone confronting a suspicious Saint Peter, as the caption explains:

> St. Peter, having had his orders for some time, refuses admittance to Mr. Gladstone. Mr. Gladstone then commences to speak—"It was a great effort, worthy of a great occasion," wrote the Recording Angel.

"Never had the Old Man Eloquent spoken with more fire and force, nor employed his inexhaustible resources of dialectic to greater effect." The O.M.E. is here proving that Heaven was one of his birthplaces. The simple ex-fisherman gradually falls under "the wizard spell of his eloquence" and in order to avoid the peroration, unbars the gates of gold and pearl.

Another drawing shows Gladstone addressing a mass meeting and paying "an eloquent and graceful tribute to God." Later, he is cut by the prince consort. Still later, he is aghast when he discovers that one of the heavenly streets is named Disraeli Avenue. At last, Gladstone leaves Heaven, refusing to give a tip to Saint Peter: "Certainly not! I presume you are paid your wages?" The final drawing represents Gladstone in Hell: "Peace with Sulphur. 'And one clear call for me.' "

The Gladstone series, one of Beerbohm's first attempts at a group of related drawings, is one of his best. The cumulative effect is greater than the effect of any single drawing. The challenge to public taste, though not put to the test in 1898, clearly anticipates the caricatures of royalty in 1923. When the Gladstone pictures were finally published, there was no one to be outraged. The drawings could be fully relished for their skill and wit.

III The Second Childhood of John Bull

In 1901 Beerbohm held his first exhibition in the Carfax Gallery, London. Among the hundred drawings displayed was a series of fifteen entitled "The Second Childhood of John Bull." Against the background of the Boer War, Beerbohm's political figures, underlined in long captions, were more in the boisterous style of Gillray than in the sophisticated manner usually associated with Beerbohm. When the series was published in 1911, a reviewer found the drawings too serious and obvious, and that impression is even stronger today. Better than the drawings are the captions, which contain some excellent parody.

The point of the series appears in the first two plates. The Ideal John Bull, with determined look, says, "I'm going to see this thing through"—that is the Boer War. The Real John Bull, however, takes sentimental comfort in past achievements: "Ah, well, but I ain't doin' so badly neither. There's Bony under lock an' key at St. Helena. An' Drake he have stopped that there

Armada. An' Burgoyne's goin' to teach them Colonists a lesson. Just you wait. What I say is 'Old England's old England still.'" A spider web in the background emphasizes the obsolescence of past glories. The last two plates return to this general theme. "Darby and Joan at Dover Castle" shows John Bull looking through the wrong end of a bent telescope. In the harbor is a cruiser labeled "HMS Obsolete." Britannia's triton is now an umbrella, and a small cannon on the castle wall points inland instead of out to sea. The last drawing shows "The Twentieth Century," with startled expression, "Pressing the English Rose Between the Pages of History."

The Boer War, despite eventual British victory, was a considerable blow to British pride. War arose through rivalry between Dutch citizens of the Transvaal and the British at Cape Colony. Early fighting put the small British forces on the defensive, and the sieges of Kimberley, Ladysmith, and Mafeking were prolonged. The relief of Ladysmith in March, 1900, was the occasion for great celebration in England, which Beerbohm represents by showing John Bull drunk in the gutter. Another drawing, which shows John Bull in bed, writhing in pain, bears a caption that is a parody of official optimism: "The admiration and envy of the whole civilized world has been excited by the exemplary fortitude and self-control which (and we speak in no mere spirit of vain-gloriousness) no other nation, etc. etc."

Several drawings of the series turn upon John Bull's philistine disregard of the arts. Melpomene, muse of tragedy, is shown as a servant girl, dismissed because of her gloomy face. Her companion, Thalia, muse of comedy, is admonished: "Don't let me 'ave to make any more complaints about you tryin' to get *Ideas* into your 'ead. You keep to your own station; or I cautions you, *you'll* 'ave to go too, my girl."

In the same vein is "De Arte Poetica. J. B. to R. K." John Bull is shown seated, smoking a long clay pipe; he faces Kipling, who wears a schoolboy's cap and confronts a large mug of beer. The caption is an extended parody of Kipling and that part of British character impressed by the *Barrack-Room Ballads* familiar since 1892. John Bull addresses Kipling:

Yes, I've took a fancy to you young feller. 'Tain't often I cottons to a pote, neither. 'Course there's Shakespeare. 'E was a wonder, 'E was *(sentimentally).* "Swan of Avon" *I* calls 'im. Take 'im for all in all we shall not look upon 'is likes agin. An then there was Tennyson—'im that wrote the ode to Balaclavy. 'E was a master-mind too, in 'is way. . . . But most potes ain't like that. What I say is, *they ain't wholesome.* Look at Byron! Saucy 'ound, with 'is stuck-up airs and 'is stuck-down collars and 'is oglin' o' the gals. But *I* soon sent 'im to the right about. "Outside," said I, and out 'e went. And then there was that there friend o' his, went by the name o' Shelley, 'ad to go too. Drowned hisself in a I-talian lake, and I warrant that was the fust bath 'e ever took. Most of 'em is like that—*not wholesome,* and can't keep a civil tongue i' their 'eads. You're different, you are; don't give yourself no 'aughty airs, and though you're rough (what with your swear-words and your what-nots) I will say as 'ow you've always been very civil and respec'ful to myself. You're one o' the right sort, you are. An' them little tit-bits o' information what you gives me about my Hempire—why Alf 'armsworth 'imself couldn't do it neater, I do believe. Got your banjo with you tonight? Then empty that there mug, and give us a toon.

The emphasis of "wholesomeness" is a reminder of how much Kipling owed, indirectly, to the national disgust at the Wilde scandal of 1895. Kipling's manly vigor seemed to John Bull just the proper antidote. Though Wilde's name is not mentioned in the caption, the effect of contrast is gained by reference to Byron and Shelley. Kipling's journalistic tone is neatly marked by allusion to Harmsworth, later Lord Northcliffe, who had recently launched *The Daily Mail.* The reference to the banjo links John Bull's taste with the music hall. The tone of parody in this long caption appears often in later caricatures, but the heavy-handed style of the drawings, featuring the traditional gross figure of John Bull, is rare in later work.

IV The Poets' Corner *(1904)*

Because of its literary associations, *The Poets' Corner* is probably Beerbohm's best-known collection of drawings. Professors who must teach Wordsworth's "We Are Seven" over and over discover with delight "William Wordsworth in the Lake District, at cross-purposes." The drawing shows the elderly poet, with staff and top hat, interviewing the little girl of the poem. Each is puzzled by the other. "Robert Browning, taking tea with the

Browning Society" is another favorite. The poet, seated on a pink upholstered chair, is surrounded by fifteen unsmiling figures reflecting in a variety of expressions reverence, mystification, polite boredom, and even querulous indignation. Beerbohm assumes that Browning's actual aversion to the formation of Browning societies is known to the viewer of this drawing. Byron "shaking the dust of England from his shoes" is familiar through frequent reproduction in books about Byron. Kipling is touched more lightly than in the John Bull plate. Britannia, dressed as a Greek goddess, and Kipling, blowing a small trumpet, have changed headgear: the goddess wears a derby; Kipling, a classic helmet. The caption reads "Mr. Rudyard Kipling takes a bloomin' day aht, on the blasted 'eath, along with Britannia, 'is gurl."

The first plate of the twenty in the series is "Omar Khayyam," a witty deflation of the romantic self-indulgence familiar in FitzGerald's popular translation. Omar, so fat he must be shown lying down, reads from a tiny pink book ("1—The Book of Verses"). Other items in the famous stanza are duly ticketed: the bough, the loaf of bread, the jug of wine, Thou (an unattractive female yawning in neglect), and "Wilderness," the endless sandy desert.

There is no sequence to the twenty drawings. Omar is followed by Browning, Goethe, Arnold, Ibsen, Byron, and Whitman. Most of the figures are of the nineteenth century, but Shakespeare is shown receiving the manuscript of *Hamlet* from Francis Bacon; a many-headed Homer, symbolizing the dispute over his identity, strums his lyre; and Dante in Oxford is interrogated by a proctor who asks the usual question, "Your name and college?" Representation of the nineteenth century is in no way complete. Tennyson, reading *In Memoriam* to Queen Victoria, both figures dwarfed by a spacious palace room, is one of the best known. Around Dante Gabriel Rossetti "in his back-garden" are gathered Swinburne, Meredith, Morris, and other associates. Coleridge talks at the head of a table to a pyramid of snoring companions. Scott, Keats, and Shelley are notably absent from the series. Walt Whitman is the only American; he is shown performing an awkward dance in front of an American eagle, "inciting the bird of freedom to soar."

V A Book of Caricatures *(1907)*

Based on the successful Carfax Gallery exhibition of 1907, *A Book of Caricatures* included forty-nine drawings of political, literary, and artistic celebrities. Many of these people are now forgotten, or very dimly remembered; but the drawings emphasize types of behavior so broadly recognizable that biographical ignorance does not preclude enjoyment. The reader unacquainted with W. J. Locke's *The Beloved Vagabond,* a popular novel of 1906, may still relish Beerbohm's representation of him taking tea, surrounded by five admiring ladies in merry-widow hats. Although the reader may never have encountered the name of Henry Chaplin, who died in 1923, and may not remember his fame as huntsman and country gentleman member of parliament, the huge overcoated figure of Beerbohm's drawing, and the serious, self-confident expression on his small face immediately associate him with his later counterparts. At the same time, there is a curious reminder of Chaplin's period: exact counterparts of Mr. Henry Chaplin no longer exist.

"Sir Hedworth Williamson approaching the Presence" in court costume, handing hat and gloves to two liveried servants, is part of Beerbohm's recurrent irony at the expense of royalty. "Mr. Claude Lowther dominating Paris" is a great figure sartorially imposing in large collar and cuffs, towering over Paris streets; his confident smile suggests the exact English temperament that has always found it impossible to understand the French. A similar point is made in the same way in a drawing of Sir William Eden.

For anyone who turns the pages of this volume, however, the familiar figures give most pleasure. "Mr. H. G. Wells, prophet and idealist, conjuring up the darling Future" presents the graceless, stocky figure of Wells as he contemplates a woman holding a precocious infant. "Mr. Hilaire Belloc striving to win Mr. Gilbert Chesterton over from the errors of Geneva" reveals a gesticulating Belloc standing on a chair to lecture the gross, overfed Chesterton on religious doctrine. Mr. Bernard Shaw, his beard Mephistophelean, stands with scaly tail draped over one arm. "Mr. Sargent at Work," the frontispiece, dashes at his canvas, a brush in each hand, to immortalize an ermine-draped society woman; in the foreground, a string trio provides inspiration. In another drawing, young Winston Churchill, head thrust forward, aggressively confronts the future.

Two drawings of Henry James include captions that parody the Master's style as skillfully as the two well-known essays previously discussed. In the first, "London in November and Mr. James in London," James endeavors to see his hand before his face in a fog: ". . . It was, therefore, not without something of a shock that he, in this to him so very congenial atmosphere, now perceived that a vision of the hand which he had, at a venture, held up within an inch or so of his eyes, was, with an almost awful clarity, being adumbrated. . . ."

In the second, "Mr. Henry James visiting America," the following "extract from unspoken thoughts" is given: ". . . So that, in fine, let, without further beating about the bush, me make to myself amazed acknowledgment that, but for the certificate of birth which I have, so very indubitably *on* me, I might, in regarding, and, as it somewhat were, overseeing, *à l'oeil de voyageur,* these dear good people, find hard to swallow, or even to take by subconscious injection, the great idea that I am—oh, ever so indigenously!—one of them. . . ." The parenthesis interrupting "let me make," the colloquial "beating about the bush," the "somewhat" added to "as it were," the French phrase—these are all immediately recognizable exaggerations of Jamesian mannerisms. Nine figures in the background represent American types as different as possible from James. A girl calls out: "My! ain't he cree-ative?" An Indian welcomes James: "Hail great white novelist! Turiyaba—the spinner of fine cobwebs!" A group of four give an American college yell: "What's the matter with—James? He's all—right! *Who's* all right? James."

Three drawings satirize Beerbohm's artist friends. "Mr. Walter Sickert explaining away Piazza San Marco" presents Sickert in shapeless jacket and wide-brimmed hat averting his gaze from the Doge's palace at the far end of the great square in Venice. "Chelsea and Mr. Steer, by moonlight" gives us the south bank of the Thames River as background, dwarfed by the rounded bulk of Philip Wilson Steer, whose tiny head perches at the top of an immense overcoat. "Some Members of the New English Art Club" includes a dozen figures, all unnamed. Steer is in the center, a large figure on a small chair; from a table nearby the diminutive Will Rothenstein lectures him.

VI *Popularity as Caricaturist*

When Beerbohm married and went to Italy in 1910, he had established himself as a distinguished caricaturist. The volumes of 1896, 1904, and 1907 were given added importance by exhibitions at the Carfax Gallery in London in 1901, 1904, 1907, and 1908. In these years 226 drawings were exhibited, as compared with the 94 in the three published collections. Between 1896 and 1910 more than a hundred caricatures appeared in a variety of magazines, notably *The Idler, The Academy, The World, The Bookman, John Bull,* and two American publications, the Chicago *Chapbook,* and *The Critic.* Also important in establishing Beerbohm's reputation were the dozens of drawings dashed off and distributed to admiring and influential friends.

It is, therefore, not surprising that Beerbohm received in 1910 an advance payment for an exhibition to be held at the Leicester Gallery in London in 1911. How much Beerbohm's drawings had profited him up to 1910 is uncertain. He speaks of selling early drawings to *Pick-Me-Up* at a guinea and a half (about $7.50). The Gladstone drawings of 1898, sold to a private collector, brought a little less. In 1911 the original drawings of John Bull sold for fifty pounds (about $250), and Beerbohm considered the price low.[11]

During Beerbohm's retirement, and particularly during the 1920's, his fame and profits as caricaturist were greatest. There were London exhibitions at the Leicester Gallery in 1911, 1913, 1921 (both spring and fall), 1923, 1925, and 1928; these exhibitions included nearly four hundred drawings. In 1911 Beerbohm wrote Turner that sales had amounted to seven hundred pounds ($3,500), and he expected a total of a thousand pounds. In 1913 he cleared over twelve hundred pounds; in 1921, eleven hundred pounds.[12]

Such sales naturally increased the demand for the volumes of drawings Beerbohm published in 1913, 1921, 1922, 1923, and 1925. Only about a thousand copies of *A Book of Caricatures* (1907) had been printed. In 1913, the first printing of three thousand copies was followed the next year by another thousand copies. In 1921, there were five thousand copies of *A Survey;* in 1922, thirty-five hundred of *Rossetti and His Circle.* There were smaller printings of *Things New and Old* (1923) and of *Observa-*

tions (1925), but prices were higher, about six dollars for each volume.

Beerbohm's financial affairs have never been clearly described, but it is likely that he made far more from his drawings than from his writings. After 1925, however, he drew only for his own pleasure, saying that caricature was a young man's game. This decision is a major reason for the genteel poverty of Beerbohm's later years.

VII *Later Volumes: Literary Subjects*

With one exception, the five volumes of caricatures published between 1913 and 1925 are assortments of literary, artistic, and political personalities, with some drawings which make general social comment. Since detailed discussion of each volume is beyond the scope of this chapter, it is convenient to illustrate first the treatment of literature and art. Because of its special quality and content, *Rossetti and His Circle* (1922) is separately discussed.

In the 1913 volume, easily the best literary caricature is that of Shaw standing on his head (described at the beginning of this chapter). Publication of John Masefield's *The Widow in the Bye Street* (1912) gave point to a drawing of the poet looking over the tenement houses of a group of quarreling neighbors. Below is the caption: "A swear-word in a rustic slum/ A simple swear-word is to some/ To Masefield nothing more." Frequently reproduced is "Mr. Thomas Hardy Composing a Lyric." On the dark heath an owl sits in a gnarled tree; in the foreground, Hardy, a large head on a tiny body, looks very wistful. Joseph Pennell, biographer and apologist for James McNeill Whistler, is drawn in the familiar pose of Whistler's mother, "thinking of the old 'un." The art critic Roger Fry inspects a miniature statue and announces pretentiously: "We must needs love the highest when we see it." In each of these drawings, the caption is essential in deflating self-importance. Other drawings are devoted to George Moore and Arnold Bennett; and, from Continental Europe, to D'Annunzio, Hauptmann, Rodin, and Caruso.

The 1921 volume is less literary in emphasis than one might expect. Joseph Conrad had been on the literary scene since 1895, but two drawings reflect his postwar vogue. In the frontispiece, Conrad views a green snake writhing in a skull that lies on a sandy beach. Conrad, impeccably dressed and wearing a monocle, comments: "What a delightful coast! One catches the illusion that one might forever be almost gay here." The second drawing shows Conrad striding into a literary gathering: "A Party in the Parlour, 'all silent and all damned,' and, as usual, Mr. Conrad intruding"—a reference to Conrad's inflammable temper. Shaw, a favorite subject, is now trying to pawn his clothing to Georg Brandes, the Danish literary critic. When Brandes objects that the coat is really Schopenhauer's, the waistcoat Ibsen's, and the trousers Nietzsche's, Shaw triumphantly replies: "Ah, but look at the patches." Like Conrad and Shaw, writers such as Maurice Hewlett, George Moore, Edmund Gosse, Hilaire Belloc, who are shown in other drawings, were familiar figures in prewar England. The only new literary name in the volume is Lytton Strachey, who is contriving to see Queen Victoria through the eyes of Lord Melbourne.

In 1923, Aldous Huxley, "A luminary of the Younger Generation," is shown tall, stooped, and languid. In another drawing, Osbert and Sacheverell Sitwell have parrots, perched on their wrists, who are calling "Bravo, Sacheverell," and "Well done, Osbert." "English Fiction, Ancient" is contrasted with "English Fiction, Modern": in former days, the hero tried to control a guilty passion; now he tries to muster up a guilty passion. For an ailing English drama, Dr. Granville-Barker prescribes, coached from the rear by such playwrights as Henry Arthur Jones and Shaw and by such critics as A. B. Walkley and William Archer.

Comment on the contemporary literary scene was not much extended in the 1925 volume. It is the shade of Byron who dominates the dean of Westminster and congratulates him on his refusal in 1924 (the centenary of Byron's death) to allow Byron to be memorialized in Poets' Corner: "Mr. Dean, you're a man of sense and pluck. You've defied all England, just as *I* did; and you've saved me from the company of that damned old noodle, Mr. Wordsworth." "Some Persons of the Nineties" is direct reminiscence, called forth by the publication of Osbert Burdett's *The Beardsley Period* (1925). The florid Oscar Wilde presides in the background; in the foreground, Will Rothenstein talks to Beerbohm and Beardsley. Eight other figures, including Richard Le Gallienne and George Moore, are shown. It is evident that by 1925 Beerbohm was less and less moved to caricature the strictly contemporary.

VIII Rossetti and His Circle *(1922)*

Connoisseurs regard *Rossetti and His Circle* as the very best of Beerbohm's art in caricature. His subjects—Dante Gabriel Rossetti, Swinburne, and Morris—required great versatility; and the sensitive blues, reds, and yellows—so important in the paintings of the Pre-Raphaelites themselves—are used with skill. It is a pity that these fine drawings often require more detailed knowledge of literary and artistic matters of the 1850's and 1860's than is now likely to be common. Even in 1922 Beerbohm anticipated that ignorance would prevent appreciation of his drawings. "Perhaps you have never heard of Rossetti," he remarks in his prefatory Note; but, he continues, "even you . . . must have heard of the Victorian era. Rossetti belonged to that —though he was indeed born nine years before it began, and died of it nineteen years before it was over. For him the eighteen-fifties-and-sixties had no romance at all. For me, I confess, they are very romantic—partly because I wasn't alive then, and partly because Rossetti was." Beerbohm then ranks Rossetti with Byron and Disraeli as the most interesting men of the nineteenth century—the most interesting because the most complex. Rossetti, in the midst of industrial complacency, shone, for those who knew him, "with the ambiguous light of a red torch somewhere in a dense fog. And so he still shines for me."

Dante Gabriel Rossetti (1828–82), the son of an Italian expatriate, became well known as painter and poet. He was the leading spirit of the Pre-Raphaelite Brotherhood, whose paintings in the 1850's evoked a brooding, emotional intensity. This mood was intended to suggest the creative period of Italian art before Raphael's manner became the convention of art schools and critics. The eloquent John Ruskin championed the Brotherhood against attacks by established artists and critics. Later, Rossetti's poems, such as "The Blessed Damozel," achieved similar haunting melancholy. Rossetti, a moody, intense man, attracted to himself such painters as William Holman Hunt and John Everett Millais and such poets as A. C. Swinburne and William Morris. Morris's fondness for medieval crafts was greatly stimulated by association with Rossetti. Rossetti's sister Christina wrote lyrics of great beauty, and a brother, William Michael, was a painter, poet, literary critic, and biographer.

Besides the undeniable talent of the Pre-Raphaelites, the Brotherhood attracted attention by two sensational episodes. In 1854 Ruskin's marriage was legally dissolved, and his wife later married Millais. In 1862, Rossetti's wife died from an overdose of laudanum; and Rossetti, in a paroxysm of grief, buried with her the only manuscript of a number of his poems. Later, the manuscript was disinterred, and the poems were published in 1870. The Pre-Raphaelites, with their esthetic and emotional emphasis, were a major influence on Whistler and Oscar Wilde, and in turn on Beerbohm, Beardsley, and others in the 1890's.

When Beerbohm settled in Rapallo, he decorated the hall of his house with frescoes of Rossetti and his friends. During the war years with the Rothensteins in England, he began the drawings which were exhibited in September, 1921, and published the following year. They combine the sympathetic affection and awe which Beerbohm felt in his youth for the Pre-Raphaelites, with the amused sense of their oddity which was part of his later response.

Of the twenty-two plates, a few are clear with a minimum of explication. In one, Mr. Browning "brings a lady of fashion and rank to see Mr. Rossetti." It is evident from the distinguished air of Browning and the lady, and from Browning's thumb extended in the direction of the corpulent Rossetti, that the Pre-Raphaelite inhabits a world different from that of his visitors. Yet it is an artistic world, as is evident in the wainscotted wall, the blue paper above set off by white china plates. In another drawing Rossetti shows his plainly dressed sister Christina fabrics of nine different shades and tries to persuade her to select one for a dress: "What is the use, Christina, of having a heart like a singing bird and a watershoot and all the rest of it, if you insist on getting yourself up like a pew-opener?"

The mystical character of Rossetti's work is whimsically highlighted when John Morley introduces John Stuart Mill to Rossetti with the suggestion that the artist illustrate Mill's *Subjection of Women*. The rationalistic Mill, manfully protesting the traditional mistreatment of women, lived in a world as far as possible from that of the visionary Rossetti. Another intimation of Rossetti's special quality is a riverside scene in which Swinburne is taking his new friend Edmund Gosse to meet Rossetti. The tiny Swinburne, his flying red hair crowned by a topper, is followed by the bespectacled Gosse, book in hand. What will the quietly studious Gosse make of the moody, flamboyant Rossetti? The last drawing in the collection bears this caption: "The name of Dante Gabriel Rossetti is heard for the first time in America. Time: 1881. Lecturer: Mr. Oscar Wilde." Wilde is shown in kneebreeches, velvet jacket, and flowing tie; in his hand he holds a lily. His face is flabby, but his hair, usually drawn by Beerbohm as a disorderly swirl, is here a neat bob. The hard-faced, gray-clad listeners, the grim platform guests, and an unattractive portrait of Lincoln on the wall create a singularly alien atmosphere for Wilde and Rossetti.

IX *Political and Social Topics*

Many of the political caricatures require detailed knowledge of the careers of men not now well remembered, but often the general point is clear enough. In the 1913 volume, "Mr. Balfour —A Frieze" is one of Beerbohm's purely visual effects. The tall figure is drawn five times, each time with the head held a little higher, until in the last drawing the hat falls off, a literal reminder of the risks in Balfour's conspicuous high-mindedness. "Mr. Asquith in Office" shows the new prime minister beset by Germany, Labour, and other problems; Asquith sits placid in the spirit of the quotation below: "Come one, come all, this rock shall fly/ From its firm base as soon as I."

In the 1921 volume the threat of a Labour government looms. The departure of the French ambassador is explained in a prophetic picture captioned: "When Labour Rules, or, what M. Cambon Frightfully Foresees, and why M. Cambon is leaving us." A burly Labourite in sack coat holds out an oversized hand to the French ambassador, bearded, formally dressed, and holding his silk hat behind him. The rest of the caption explains the scene: "Secretary for Foreign Affairs (holding his first weekly reception): 'Glad to see you Moosoo! You'll find I'm pretty well up in all the main points already. Capital o' France: Paris, pronounced Paree. Republican form o' government, founded 1792. Principal exports: wines, silks, and woollen goods. Battle o' Waterloo, 1814. The Great War, 1914 to 1918. Take a chair.' "

Ramsay MacDonald, who was prime minister for a few months in 1924, is shown confronting a wall of rocks representing his insoluble problems. "Somehow," he complains, "I never noticed these things at the end of my garden." Stanley Baldwin, his Tory successor, thoughtfully remarks as he sits in an armchair under a reading lamp "Back at Chequers": "Vision!—that's what's wanted nowadays: vision. I must try and see if I can't—well, *see* something."

A number of drawings are more social than political. One in the 1913 volume shows the newly crowned George V in "Duties and Diversions of this Sweeter, Simpler Reign." In an effort to reestablish respectability for the royal family after the death of Edward VII, the new monarch inspects a school for infants. As has been mentioned, the series of drawings of the royal family, exhibited in 1923, drew such unfavorable comments that Beerbohm suggested the offending pictures be removed. One of these, much in the manner of the early Gladstone series, showed Edward twanging a harp in heaven, a too broad reminder of his unsaintly conduct on earth. When Beerbohm prepared the volume based on the exhibition of 1923, he retained one of the milder drawings, "The Rare, the Rather Awful Visits of Albert Edward, Prince of Wales, to Windsor Castle." The Prince stands in a corner, like a naughty boy; Queen Victoria sits in the foreground, sadly pensive over the scolding she has just administered. On the wall is the lower part of a portrait, showing only the legs of some royal personage—no doubt Edward's saintly father, Prince Albert.

The narrowness of class differences is depicted in "A Study in Assimilation" (1913). Two figures of 1868 show marked differences in costume and bearing; their twentieth-century counterparts are indistinguishable in their ungainly sprawling figures and the duplicate cigarettes that hang from their mouths. In another drawing (1913), Lord Northcliffe, creator of the sensational press in England, calls excitedly to his assistants: "Help! Again I feel the demons of Sensationalism rising in me. Hold me fast! Curb me, if you love me!" In 1925 a statesman of the olden time, translating Virgil's *Georgics,* is contrasted with one of modern times, dictating an article for his series, "Men I've Been Up Against," for seventy-five pounds a line, "grammar and style touched up in the office."

To commemorate the International Advertising Convention, Beerbohm suggests a fresco design. Ten portly figures in morning coats and sanctimonious expressions seem rapt in prayer. In the foreground a little figure labeled "Press" doffs his hat in profound respect. At the top are such slogans as "All for Each" and "Each for All." Elsewhere, the pretension of altruism in the class struggle is neatly punctured (1925) when a young working-class man looks at a portrait of the Duke of Wellington and comments: "Now that's the kind of class-consciousness *I*'d like ter have!"

In these later volumes are a number of drawings in series. On the whole, they are less clever than the Gladstone series of 1898, and only now and then do they achieve the quality of the best individual caricatures. In 1913 Beerbohm represented the twentieth century running by in an ugly motoring costume, and it is watched by the nineteenth century "with grave misgivings" and by the eighteenth century "with wicked amusement." In 1921, the eighteenth century, in wig, brocaded coat and knee-breeches, sees the future as a more sober, more pensive replica of itself. The nineteenth century, bespectacled and robust, extends a hand to an even more robust future. The twentieth century, slender, serious, and wearing a band of mourning for the war dead, confronts a question mark.

In 1923, a series of nine drawings represents the fluctuations of power in Germany, France, and England since 1815. In 1919, for example, England and France together strike a noble pose and denounce the fallen Germany. In 1923, England has returned to the desk of business as usual, leaving France and Germany to glower at each other. The series is a more restrained, and even a more thoughtful, attempt at the kind of effect gained in the John Bull drawings of the Boer War. But the points are too obvious, and the treatment is too labored to show Beerbohm at his best.

"Studies in the Eighteen-Seventies," in the same volume, is a different kind of series. Playfully put forth as the work of the artist at the age of five, these drawings of imaginary figures represent Beerbohm's impressions of adult life during his childhood. General Sir George Rawlins, V.C.G.C.M.G., etc., is a perennial military type. He is "convinced, rightly or wrongly, that the abolition of the purchase system [for army commissions] must entail the instant surrender of England to whatever foreign power will attack her."

The best of these attempts at related comments is a series of 1925 entitled "The Young and the Old Self." In the eighteen drawings of the series, the idea proved flexible and congenial. With the perspective gained from thirty years of close observation of English life, Beerbohm was able to make telling contrasts between the expectations of youth and the realities of late middle age. In the beautifully tinted frontispiece, Arthur Balfour is shown lying languidly on a green sofa at Oxford, where his greatest wish was to spend his life in the study of philosophy. When his old self appears, jauntily dressed for tennis, the young man is unimpressed by the venerable statesman: "Who are you? You look rather like Uncle Salisbury, shaved. And what is that curious thing you're holding? . . . But don't answer: I don't really care. And don't let me talk: I don't fancy I've long to live; and I want to devote my time to thinking—not that I suppose my thought has much value, but—oh do, please, go away."

The young self of H. G. Wells alludes briefly to his scientific studies: "Did you ever manage to articulate the bones of that microglamaphoid lizard?" To this question the old self replies: "I'm not sure. But I've articulated the whole past of mankind on this planet—and the whole future, too. I don't think you know very much about the past, do you? It's all perfectly beastly, believe me. But the future's going to be perfectly splendid—after a bit. And I must say I find the present very jolly." George Moore's old self shyly admits to his young self that, since Balzac, there has been only one real novelist—obviously himself. In one of the best of Beerbohm's comments on Shaw, the sage of 1925 confronts the vigorous young self of the 1890's: "Strange! You strike me as frivolous, irreligious, and pert; full of a ludicrous faith in mankind and in the efficacy of political propaganda, squalidly needy in circumstances, and abominably ill-dressed. . . . And I used to think you quite perfect!"

X *Achievement in Caricature*

After 1925 Beerbohm drew little, published little, exhibited seldom. In 1931 five drawings of characters in Noel Coward's musical comedy appeared as *Heroes and Heroines of Bitter Sweet*, but they are not caricatures. The little volume was a friendly gesture to Noel Coward and, as the defensive Note states, a tribute to the enduring appeal of sentiment, despite "the roarings of young lions and lionesses of Bloomsbury." The exhibition of 1928, entitled "Ghosts," was a selection of 109 previously exhibited drawings of important personalities. In 1952, "'Max' in Retrospect" included 152 drawings, only two of them dated after 1932. Though Beerbohm helped to plan this exhibition, he could not return to England to attend it. In the catalogue he stated that he had ceased to draw when he realized that he "was no longer seeing people in terms of caricature." [13]

The collections published by Beerbohm include 338 drawings. To this total *Max's Nineties*, for which Beerbohm made suggestions, adds thirty-nine. The catalogues of exhibitions list more than six hundred drawings, many of them, of course, later included in the published volumes. In preparation is a complete catalogue of the more than eighteen hundred known drawings. When this work appears, it will be possible to trace in detail Beerbohm's development and to evaluate with some exactness his very considerable achievement.

It will also be possible to make new selections and new groupings of Beerbohm's varied work. To the familiar drawings of literary figures must be added a sketch which imaginatively records the luncheon meeting in 1923 of Thomas Hardy and the Prince of Wales (now the Duke of Windsor). When Beerbohm heard that arrangements had been made for the prince to call on the aging novelist and poet, he sent Hardy his impression of the event. The writer is drawn standing, in a mood of frail apprehension. Through the door bounces the smiling prince. The caption completes the effect: "Mayn't I call you Tom?" [14]

On the basis of the well-known collections, it can be said that the most notable quality of Beerbohm as caricaturist is his grace. Only occasionally, as in the Boer War series, is the touch heavy. Usually, even when the figure represented is unknown to the viewer, or dimly remembered, there is a grace of line that catches the attention. Beerbohm's drawings are beautiful without being prettified. He was moved to caricature by what he considered pretentious or eccentric. The pretentiousness of Wilde and Shaw, however, did not cancel their genius, and this recognition is what we feel as we look at Beerbohm's drawings. Few men can have been more eccentric than Dante Gabriel Rossetti, but Beerbohm's drawings suggest also his mysterious charm. As in his writing, Beerbohm speaks for the "sensible" man; he is annoyed by human inconsistencies, but never moved to the savagery of Gillray or the sentimentality of Phiz. Few of the able caricaturists who were Beerbohm's contemporaries can offer the present-day readers so much pleasure.

As has been shown in this chapter, the caricatures include some of Beerbohm's most memorable writing. As we view the drawings and read the captions we are included for a few moments in the magic circle of Beerbohm's conversation. More clearly than with most writers, it was Beerbohm's talk that was the basis for his success not only as essayist, dramatic critic, and novelist, but as caricaturist. The best talk is at once spontaneous and compressed by wit and imagination. The best captions in the caricatures are excellent talk.

CHAPTER 7

Evaluation

NO one has ever considered Max Beerbohm a "major" literary figure, whatever that nebulous term may mean. Surely he never saw himself as a Milton, thundering from some secluded mountain top of meditation. Dr. Johnson, a somewhat Miltonic figure on occasion, once advised Boswell to clear his mind of cant; and young Beerbohm, born in 1872, when there was a good deal of cant around, set out to clear his mind of it. In the long run, and it was a very long run for him, he succeeded. This statement is the best answer to the questions: was he conservative, was he anti-democratic? In his youth, he mocked aristocracy and royalty; in later years, he mocked Labour, socialism, and the worship of the Common Man.

Like his older friend Henry James, Beerbohm was shocked that the seemingly civilized world in which he had grown up could lead to the brutalities of the 1914–18 war. Yet the word "gentleman" continued to be for him an honorable term, and he himself exemplified some of its best connotations. Leisure was natural and enjoyable to him, but he could work hard and well. He preferred genteel poverty to exploiting himself, as he showed in refusing a lucrative offer to make a television appearance.[1] He could accept with dignity the public criticism of his drawings of royalty in 1923. His friendships were numerous and warm, and they were little marred by flattery or by ill temper. He was one of the most sophisticated men of his time, superior to most popular enthusiasms and prejudices; yet he indulged an old-fashioned sentiment for Oxford, for the Pre-Raphaelites, and, in later years, for England itself.

At present, a romantic haze invests the period of Beerbohm's youth, just as a strong fascination drew him to the 1850's. Beerbohm would be the first to insist that Aubrey Beardsley was a far greater artist that he, yet the drawings of Beerbohm have a range of interest far greater, and less dated, than Beardsley's. In Beerbohm's drawings the great literary and political figures of his day appear to us with a humorous interpretation seldom found in textbooks. No one can be said to "know" the turn of the century who has not looked repeatedly at such a selection as *Max's Nineties* affords.

As an essayist, Beerbohm will be fair game for anthologists as long as essays are valued, and selections from him are bright pages in any volume. Of the hundred or so which Beerbohm collected, S. C. Roberts selected thirty-three for his volume *The Incomparable Max*. Every reader of the original collections could make a few additions and deletions from the Roberts volume; but, as it stands, *The Incomparable Max* is an achievement as distinctive and as durable as Lamb's *Essays of Elia* or as Thackeray's *Roundabout Papers*.

Of *Zuleika Dobson*, it is hard to make a prediction. As Oxford itself loses more and more of its nineteenth-century character, Beerbohm's story becomes more and more dated, as do drawings that show the university as it was in 1800. Even so, the theme of the story, its structure, and, above all, its style, invite the appreciation of the knowing.

About 1894 Oscar Wilde remarked that upon Max Beerbohm the gods had bestowed the gift of perpetual old age. In 1898, Shaw welcomed "the incomparable Max" as his successor on the staff of *The Saturday Review*. There is truth in both of these oft-repeated judgments, yet they obscure an important part of the truth. Beerbohm's career was not, as these comments imply, all of a piece. Both as caricaturist and as writer, he developed from the bumptious undergraduate to the self-assured essayist of *And Even Now* (1920) and to the exhibitor of caricatures between 1921 and 1925. When Beerbohm published *Works* and *Twenty-five Gentlemen* in 1896, he was straining to attract attention. Clever as he was in "The Pervasion of Rouge," and "King George the Fourth," the skill required for *Zuleika Dobson, Seven Men,* and the best of *And Even Now* lay far ahead.

The twelve-year stint as dramatic critic for *The Saturday Review* Beerbohm accepted with reluctance and gave up with relief. And it is true that his weekly essays, good as they are, seldom if ever reach the level of his best free-lance writing. On the whole, however, the post of dramatic critic was fortunate. It required regular writing, and it kept constantly before Beerbohm the problems of theme, character, structure, and style. Within limits, his position required and nourished independence. In no clearly definable sense is there development in Beerbohm's criticism. A late article on Shaw or Shakespeare would be difficult to distinguish from an early one. Yet Beerbohm was a different man in 1910 from what he had been in 1898, and his experience on *The Saturday Review* is part of the difference.

I *"I Am Not Incomparable"*

In 1921, Beerbohm himself made the best appraisal of his own career. When his younger friend, the novelist and caricaturist Bohun Lynch, wrote the first book about him, Beerbohm politely refused assistance; but in a letter he made this self-evaluation: "My gifts are small. I've used them very well and discreetly, never straining them; and the result is that I've made a charming little reputation." He then challenged Shaw's epithet:

> Note that I am *not* incomparable. Compare me. Compare me as essayist (for instance) with other essayists. Point out how much less human I am than Lamb, how much less intellectual than Hazlitt, and what an ignoramus I am beside Belloc; and how Chesterton's high spirits and abundance shame me; how unbalanced G. S. Street must think me, and how coarse, too; and how much lighter E. V. Lucas' touch is than mine; and so on, and so forth. Apply the comparative method to me also as a caricaturist. Tend rather to *under*rate me—so that those who don't care for my work shall not be incensed, and those who do shall rally round me.[2]

So shrewd a self-estimate underlines the evidence in the work itself: it was intelligent effort that developed the undergraduate skill of 1893 into the perfection of 1920—a limited perfection, to be sure, but still perfection.

Beerbohm served his own generation extremely well. He succeeded as essayist, staff critic of drama, novelist, parodist, and caricaturist. His achievements in these different capacities are held together by acute common sense, unsentimental whimsy, and a sense of beauty fresh and individual. Above all, he was a stylist who made himself heard without shouting. Beside Beerbohm, many of his contemporaries sound shrill, like Shaw and Chesterton; or bustling, like Wells and Bennett; or precious, like Wilde, Yeats, and Conrad. And, as we have seen, Beerbohm's verbal skill gave many of his caricatures a subtle italics that better draughtsmen could seldom supply.

II *Style*

In an early uncollected article, Beerbohm shows that he carefully considered the problem of style. Without a style, he thought, writing is nothing. Writing is essentially talking without the aid of gesture, facial expression, and "the infinitely variable pauses of the human voice."[3] Most of the quotations from Beerbohm in previous pages of this book create the illusion of ideas spoken rather than written. Particularly is this true when we read the captions of the caricatures, for the character shown seems to be thinking aloud, as when Stanley Baldwin is made to say: "I must try and see if I can't—well, *see* something." Or Beerbohm himself adds a comment, as if he were standing beside us: Byron is "shaking the dust of England from his shoes"; Whitman is "inciting the bird of freedom to soar."

Beerbohm's style can be more easily illustrated than described or analyzed. Of modern writers, he is one of the most quotable. He is simple and clear without dropping into platitude. He has stronger feeling than his reputation as a wit suggests, but the play of fancy checks the self-indulgence which is sentimentality. Above all, he has an ear sensitive to the sound of language. When Harold Nicolson misquoted Churchill's most famous sentence, Beerbohm wrote the *Spectator* to object: Nicolson's version, "never have so many owed so much to so few," Beerbohm said, was "joggety-jogget and tumpty-tum." In contrast, Churchill's actual words, "never has so much been owed by so many to so few," had "a noble and classic cadence."[4]

Much has been made of Beerbohm's fondness for unusual words. He introduces archaisms like "misprision," "orgulous," and "perpend"; odd forms like "lightlier," "somewhy," and "thenabouts"; coinages such as "dryasdustocracy" and "snippetismus"; and extended hyphenations like "his for-a-brief-while-brother-manager."[5] Though an imposing list of such peculiarities has been compiled from the whole body of Beerbohm's writings, the actual occurrence of unusual words is only occasional. In context, they are almost always clear. Even when the individual word remains odd rather than clever, the attempt to escape triteness is welcome, and the reader's sense of the resources of the language is enriched. The playfulness with which unusual words are introduced adds a diverting grace note to standard English. The context is handled with such precision and beauty that a tone of authority is quietly established.

As a sample passage to illustrate Beerbohm's capacity to "talk" in print, let us take almost—but not quite—at random, the first paragraph of "Laughter," written in 1920 and included in *And Even Now:*

> M. Bergson, in his well-known essay on this theme, says . . . well, he says many things; but none of these, though I have just read them, do I clearly remember, nor am I sure that in the act of reading I understood any of them. That is the worst of these fashionable philosophers—or rather, the worst of me. Somehow I never manage to read them till they are just going out of fashion, and even then I don't seem able to cope with them. About twelve years ago, when every one suddenly talked to me about Pragmatism and William James, I found myself moved by a dull but irresistible impulse to try Schopenhauer, of whom, years before that, I had heard that he was the easiest reading in the world, and the most exciting and amusing. I wrestled with Schopenhauer for a day or so, in vain. Time passed; M. Bergson appeared "and for his hour was lord of the ascendant"; I tardily tackled William James. I bore in mind, as I approached him, the testimonials that had been lavished on him by all my friends. Alas, I was insensible to his thrillingness. His gaiety did not make me gay. His crystal clarity confused me dreadfully. I could make nothing of William James. And now, in the fullness of time, I have been floored by M. Bergson.[6]

In this paragraph Beerbohm achieves a number of his typical effects. He begins as if he were going to give a conventional summary of Bergson's "well-known" essay. He interrupts himself, however, as he might in conversation, to tell the honest truth. He cannot remember what Bergson said, and he doubts if he understood it. Condemnation of such popular but puzzling philosophers is instinctive, but, interrupting himself again, he turns the criticism against himself. The paragraph then takes a narrative turn. The earlier popularity of William James led Beerbohm to try Schopenhauer, unsuccessfully; the popularity of Bergson led him to James, in vain; and now Bergson has disappointed him. The perversity of his experience is engaging.

The skill and literateness of the paragraph attest to Beerbohm's competence as a judge. We hardly believe his assertion that he cannot understand these philosophers. The implication is, rather, that they are not worth comprehending; at least, their reputations must be inflated. In the guise of humility, Beerbohm has just stricken three "great books" from the hard-pressed reader's list, and the reader is grateful.

Several verbal felicities sharpen the effect of the paragraph. On hearing the praise of William James, Beerbohm has a "dull but irresistable impulse" to read Schopenhauer, but this reaction was better than yielding, sheeplike, to the insistence of his friends that he read James. "Time passed" and the solemnly quoted "lord of the ascendant" suggest the approach of some dramatic climax. The pattern is repeated: praise of Bergson has driven Beerbohm at last to James. The disappointment in James is a series of clichés, revitalized by uncompromising negatives: "I was insensitive to his thrillingness. His gaiety did not make me gay. His crystal clarity confused me dreadfully." "Thrillingness," by its unusual form, seems in itself to diminish the claim. The final sentence shifts to another pattern, but it secures a similar contrast between cliché and actuality: "And now, in the fullness of time, I have been floored by M. Bergson." The hallowed conventionality of "the fullness of time" insures the maximum effect of the slang "I have been floored."

The paragraph has the movement of good talk. The topic is developed but in no labored way. Idea and illustration blend naturally, as they do in conversation. Interruptions, sentence structure, and diction are delicately refined to supply what tone of voice and facial expression would add to speech. Beerbohm was famous for his talk before he became a writer, and through his brother Herbert, Oscar Wilde, and Will Rothenstein he early met the men and women who valued conversation as a fine art. Rothenstein ranks Beerbohm with Whistler, Wilde, Henry James, Shaw, George Moore, and Yeats as the best talkers he knew.[7] Talking—and listening—Beerbohm learned the possibilities of language. He did not record the "good things" he got off in conversation and save them for his essays, nor did he indulge in the annoying habit of quoting his own writings. The give and take, the spontaneous shift of strategy, the note of parody, the mingling of the intellectual and the colloquial that characterizes good talk he adapted to the printed page. This was the secret of his style. In the early essays, and in *Zuleika Dobson,* there is sometimes an exaggerated straining for effect. In later writings, as in the paragraph from "Laughter," the effects are better because they appear more natural.

III *Later Inactivity*

Praise of Beerbohm's achievements, however enthusiastic, must take note of the relative inactivity of his later years. He lived on, in reasonably good health, until 1956, but, had he died in 1925, we should have nearly all the work by which he is remembered. Even of the radio talks delivered after 1935, at least two were written as early as 1913, and would have survived in manuscript. The other radio talks, the fine lecture about Lytton Strachey in 1943, and S. N. Behrman's record of Beerbohm's lively conversation when he was past eighty make clear that in the usual sense he retained his mental powers and his skill with language until the end. Between 1925 and 1956 many editors in England and America welcomed his occasional contributions, but in these years he contributed only about thirty magazine pieces, including the radio talks, later published in *The Listener.* Had Beerbohm written more, he would have found a ready market; and the income would have eased his genteel poverty. Drawing, always more of a pleasure to him than writing, was also laid aside. After 1925, Beerbohm exhibited virtually no new work; and he published only one very slight collection.

No really satisfactory explanation can be presented for the inactivity of these later years. It is sometimes argued that Beerbohm's long residence in Italy caused him to lose touch with the English public. Yet during the forty-six years after his retirement to Rapallo, Beerbohm was frequently in England; and during both wars he was there for years at a time. The work of the first fifteen years, from 1910 to 1925, is impressive: *Zuleika Dobson, Seven Men,* and *And Even Now;* and five notable collections of drawings, each preceded by a popular exhibition and by good sales. The extraordinarily successful radio talks when Beerbohm was past sixty show that he could adapt himself to a far wider public than he had reached as staff writer for *The Saturday Review.*

There is also speculation that Beerbohm's marriage to the censorious Florence diminished his creative effort. Again, the achievements during their first fifteen years together effectively refute this explanation. Nor is it much to the point to say, as some of Beerbohm's friends did, that in later years Max became lazy. His mind remained as alert as ever, and such late writings as there are show the old skill undiminished. A perverse indication of continued energy is his fondness for practical jokes that were often ingeniously witty. He relabeled the roses in the fine garden of a friend, substituting the names of criminals for rare varieties. He painstakingly removed the "h's" from a dignified poem to convert the diction to cockney and sent the volume to the author as an interesting new edition. He made dummy books, so that the visitor would seem to see *The Complete Works of Arnold Bennett* as a single slender volume. Such pranks are not the employment of a genuinely lazy man. Yet they are a little pathetic when they replace the normal outlets for proven talent.

In the Strachey lecture we find a better clue to Beerbohm's long silence. In 1900, he recalls, "I had been considered a rather clever and amusing young man. . . . In 1918 I was young no longer, and I think I amused people less than I had."[8] He implies that by the end of World War I he was losing confidence in himself. The successes of the next few years, strangely, did not restore the self-assurance of his youth; perhaps it was because he realized better than anyone else that the work of 1919 to 1925, both the writings and the drawings, were an extension of his earlier successes. Those successes could not be extended indefinitely, and at fifty he found no new directions for his talents.

When World War I began, Beerbohm was forty-two. When it was over, the world in which Beerbohm had grown up had vastly altered. Had he been involved in some part of the war effort, he might have gained new insights, but he had remained a passive spectator. Postwar England was kind to him and to his work, but the mood of the time was alien. His fondness for Thackeray, Ruskin, Swinburne, Pater, and Stevenson then seemed old-fashioned. He was not attracted to the new writers—Joyce, D. H. Lawrence, Aldous Huxley, Virginia Woolf, the Sitwells, T. S. Eliot, Proust. He was not even moved to parody them. Some old friends of prewar days—Shaw, Bennett, Galsworthy, and Maugham—enjoyed great popularity in the 1920's; but they were established playwrights and novelists. Beerbohm was neither, and he lacked their energy.

After 1925 there was a recurrent mood of self-deprecation. In 1926 Beerbohm refused an opportunity to lecture in America. He became ill at ease in social gatherings. He took a perverse pride in recalling the failure of an American edition of *Yet Again* (1909) to sell a single copy, and in the financial failure of the three-act version of *The Happy Hypocrite.* He prophesied failure for Wolcott Gibbs's attempt to dramatize *Zuleika Dobson.* Actually the 1923 American edition of *Yet Again* went into a second printing five years later, and the records of his other books show that there was a steady demand. After 1925 there were more than thirty editions of his various volumes, including an American edition of *Zuleika Dobson,* which sold forty thousand copies. Such successes, however, were extensions of Beerbohm's early fame. Indirectly, they emphasized the fact that he was publishing little or no new work.[9]

It is easy to think of projects which might have been interesting and profitable to Beerbohm in these later years. His personal story of the 1890's—Wilde, Beardsley, Shaw, Frank Harris, *The Yellow Book, The Savoy*—has been suggested in a previous chapter. Critical re-evaluations of some of his favorite writers would have been welcome, and they might have helped to bridge the gap between prewar and postwar taste. Anyone who reads "No. 2 The Pines" can speculate with pleasure on what a full-length appreciation of Swinburne might have been. "A Clergyman" suggests what Beerbohm might have done with many another passage of Boswell. A recently published letter[10] shows that Beerbohm was very fond of Trollope's novels; the revival of interest in Trollope in the 1930's would have been favorable to any discussion Beerbohm might have written. Revival of interest in James in the same period might also have led Beerbohm to collect his many scattered comments, parodies, and caricatures, and to supplement them with a fuller account of his long and intimate acquaintance with James's fiction. Beerbohm's fondness for Meredith, too, might have led to something more than "Euphemia Clashthought" and a few scattered allusions.

For several reasons Beerbohm did not attempt such projects. He had enough original and imaginative talent to consider criticism a lesser art. He had been a critic of the drama, and a close observer of his fellow critics. He remained skeptical of the critical process. He once commented: "Apparently, the habit of writing about things which he has studied, with the express intention of writing about them, destroys in a man the power of writing worthily about things in which he has delighted." [11] We can all think of exceptions, but the tension between the labor of knowledge and the spontaneity of enjoyment is real. Careful writer that he was, Beerbohm strove always to preserve the illusion of spontaneity and to appear the skillful amateur even when he had professional craft. In short essays, even on literary subjects, he succeeded admirably. He must have doubted his capacity to sustain his style and manner in longer, more systematic works. He refused, in a word, to turn from youthful brilliance to mature competence in full-scale projects.

So far as this hypothesis is true, and there is surely something in it, there is a suggestion that perhaps Beerbohm's work has been overvalued because he was so young when he did it. What valid ideas did he have, and how relevant are they today? Why could he not make the transition to the postwar world? Rothenstein once enumerated some of Beerbohm's antipathies: maps and itineraries of future life, Russian literature, Proust, cruelty to animals, D. H. Lawrence's novels, Mr. Lansbury's improvements to London, the Sankara system of Indian philosophy, and the proletarian state.[12] In short, Beerbohm had prejudices, and this is not the whole list. Moreover, he had the writing skill to make his prejudices sound authoritative.

A member of the middle class, he knew the aristocracy with some intimacy; despite its follies, he saw it as the protector of the arts which made life tolerable. He feared the increased power of Labour, yet he seems to have had little insight into the forces that caused the rise of Labour. He had what was considered a good education; he saw faults in it, but he had little interest in improving the system or in extending educational opportunity. Reverend R. L. ("Dick") Sheppard, Dean of Canterbury, whom Beerbohm met in Italy in 1929, charmed him as Sheppard did everyone; but Sheppard could never find a trace of religious speculation in him. Beerbohm scorned the vulgarity of English life, its lack of imagination, its muddleheadedness, its dullness; but in both wars, and at other times as well, he showed an instinctive and sincere patriotism.

As this record indicates, Beerbohm was no thinker. He himself would heartily agree. It was not for systematic ideas that he was valued in his own day, and his fame will endure for other reasons. So long as the late nineteenth century continues to be of interest, Beerbohm's drawings, his writings, and his early career will be indispensable comments on the age. So long as drama entertains and enlightens us, Beerbohm's dramatic criticism will speak for the discriminating and articulate playgoer. For knowing readers, his style will preserve his prejudices as well as his wisdom, and sorting the prejudices from the wisdom will be part of the fun. American readers, in particular, will find Beerbohm as independent as Thoreau and as sophisticated as *The New Yorker*—a journal which is almost inconceivable without the English precedent of the incomparable Max.

Mention of *The New Yorker* suggests that Max Beerbohm's future role will chiefly be to stimulate writers who address themselves to intelligent, lighthearted readers. Such writers will always be able to learn from Beerbohm's skill, even when he expresses prejudices no longer viable. Some readers, too, will discover Beerbohm as one of those minor writers whose work perpetuates its charm as greater figures go in and out of fashion.

Notes and References

Chapter One

1. The dates and external details of Max Beerbohm's life are well established in four works: J. G. Riewald, *Sir Max Beerbohm: A Critical Analysis with a Brief Life and a Bibliography* (The Hague, 1953); S. N. Behrman, *Portrait of Max* (New York, 1960); David Cecil, *Max, A Biography* (London, 1964); and *Max Beerbohm: Letters to Reggie Turner,* ed. Rupert Hart-Davis (London, 1964).

2. Published in *The Orient* (October, 1940); reprinted in *Letters,* pp. 293-96.

3. "Parlour Melodrama," *The Saturday Review,* October 19, 1901, pp. 494-96.

4. "From a Brother's Standpoint," *Herbert Beerbohm Tree: Some Memories of Him and His Art,* ed. Max Beerbohm (London, 1920), pp. 187-203.

5. "A Small Boy Seeing Giants," *Mainly on the Air* (London, 1946), pp. 7-36.

6. "Punch," *More* (London, 1899), p. 21.

7. *More,* pp. 153-58.

8. "Old Carthusian Memories," reprinted in *Mainly on the Air* (London, 1946), pp. 89-93.

9. Reproduced by Cecil, p. 31.

10. "Servants," *And Even Now* (London, 1920), p. 183.

11. "Hosts and Guests," *And Even Now,* pp. 137-38.

12. Charles Evans, "A Note on 'Carmen Becceriense,'" *Book Collector, I* (1952), pp. 215-16. Riewald, p. 213, reproduces the first page.

13. Charterhouse Library has many of these drawings. Bohun Lynch, *Max Beerbohm in Perspective* (London, 1921), p. 106, reproduces several.

14. A later Carthusian, Robert Graves, has left a more circumstantial account of his schooldays at Charterhouse. Though Graves attended the school a quarter century after Beerbohm, and was a boy of much more violent temperament, it is likely that the bullying, snobbery, and homosexuality he describes so vividly in *Goodbye to All That* (London, 1929), were features of the life Beerbohm knew.

15. Cecil, pp. 46-47.
16. "Diminuendo," *Works* (London, 1896), p. 151.
17. *Letters,* p. 65.
18. "Groups of Myrmidons," *More,* p. 49.
19. "The House of Commons Manner," *Yet Again,* 186-87.
20. Cecil, p. 59.
21. "H. B. Irving as a Young Man," *Mainly on the Air* (London, 1957), pp. 102-8.
22. *Letters,* p. 49.
23. "Going Back to School," *More,* p. 155.
24. *The Saturday Review,* March 11, 1905.
25. *The Saturday Review,* "Several Theatres," June 1, 1901; "Drama at Oxford," May 23, 1903; "About, and In, Oxford," July 6, 1907; "The O.U.D.S.," February 29, 1908. In contrast is his very sharp review of *Agamemnon,* captioned "Aeschylos Made Ridiculous," November 24, 1900. Cambridge, "after Oxford the most distinguished of our universities" need not "make a hopeless hash of a Greek tragedy."
26. Rupert Hart-Davis, in *Letters,* p. 10, identifies Turner as the natural son of Lionel Lawson. Left a considerable sum of money, Turner was always generous to Beerbohm; when Turner died in 1938, his will gave Beerbohm three thousand pounds. The allusion to great talkers is in a broadcast of 1936, "Speed," *Mainly on the Air* (London, 1957), p. 17. The fourth talker was Charles Brookfield, son of Thackeray's friend. Turner is said to appear as Algy in D. H. Lawrence's novel *Aaron's Rod,* chapter xvi.
27. "Enoch Soames," *Seven Men* (London, 1919), pp. 4-5.
28. *Men and Memories: Recollections of William Rothenstein 1872-1900* (New York, 1931), p. 144.
29. (London, 1896). The drawings were serially issued before that. Beerbohm was one of the four undergraduates included; the other three were athletes. Rothenstein reproduced the sketch in *Men and Memories,* p. 146.
30. Behrman, p. 56; *Letters,* p. 37, fn. 1.
31. *Patience* was orginally directed at Swinburne, but was widely interpreted as an attack on Wilde. See Frances Winwar, *Oscar Wilde and the Yellow Nineties* (New York, 1940), pp. 60-61. Wilde's lecture tour in America was the inspiration of Richard D'Oyly Carte, producer of the Gilbert and Sullivan operas (p. 71).
32. *Letters,* pp. 95, 35.
33. *Letters,* p. 73.
34. *Letters,* pp. 285-92.
35. *A Peep Into the Past* (New York, 1923). Privately printed (with facsimile of the ms.), but unauthorized. In a "Note" to *A Variety of*

Things (New York, 1928), p. ix, Beerbohm disclaims all responsibility for publication of this "squib," containing "some gibes against a distinguished writer whose life was to end in disaster." Cecil, p. 97, thinks the piece could not have been published even before the scandal.

36. *Letters,* pp. 97, 100, 102, 117, 136. The article including notice of Wilde's death was not included in Beerbohm's collection of dramatic reviews, *Around Theatres* (London, 1924).

37. Malcolm Muggeridge, "A Survivor," *New York Review of Books,* V, 8 (November 25, 1965), p. 33; see Cecil, pp. 109-10 and *Letters,* p. 171. In the same article, Muggeridge's statement that Beerbohm was a Jew ignores Cecil's circumstantial rejection of that hypothesis.

38. *Letters,* p. 48.

39. *The Green Carnation* (New York, 1894), pp. 7, 125.

40. Katherine Lyon Mix, *A Study in Yellow: The Yellow Book and Its Contributors* (University of Kansas Press, 1960), traces in interesting detail the writers associated with this magazine and *The Savoy.* Mrs. Mix quotes, p. 67, from Beerbohm's letter to her, saying that Beardsley announced the plan of *The Yellow Book* to him in late autumn, 1893.

41. "The Pervasion of Rouge," *Works,* pp. 99-124.

42. Quoted by Mix, p. 88; also by Cecil, p. 98.

43. "King George the Fourth," *Works,* pp. 59-96.

44. Harold George (pseudonym for John Harold Marston and George Ronald Wood), "Oxford at Home," *Strand Magazine,* IX (January, 1895), 109-15. The authors are identified in *Letters,* p. 56, fn. 1.

Chapter Two

1. *Letters,* pp. 97, 99, 101. Maud Tree, "Herbert and I," *Herbert Beerbohm Tree: Some Memories of Him and His Art* (London, 1920), pp. 171-80.

2. *Vanity,* February 7, 14, 21, 28, 1895. *Letters,* p. 99.

3. *Letters,* pp. 101-20, *passim.* Cecil, pp. 117-29, 218-21.

4. Cecil, pp. 221-26. *Letters,* p. 161.

5. It has been stated (Riewald, p. 19; Behrman, pp. 176-77; and Cecil, p. 229) that Florence Kahn was once Richard Mansfield's leading lady. According to *Who's Who on the Stage: 1908* (ed. Walter Browne and E. De Roy Koch, New York, 1908), her only appearance with Mansfield was the small part in *Henry V.* Early praise of her acting, such as that of Norman Hapgood, *The Stage in America* (New York, 1901), p. 175, is qualified by comments that her style of acting was inflated and old-fashioned. See *Theatre,* May, 1904, p. 112.

6. Cecil, pp. 228-41, 271-77.
7. *Around Theatres*, p. 500. William Rothenstein, *Men and Memories*, II, 175. Cecil, p. 287.
8. Cecil, pp. 286-300.
9. "An Evening of Peculiar Delirium" is a descriptive piece, with an affectation of disinterest in politics. "Press Notices of 'Punch and Judy' " is an amusing parody of the pontifical styles of reviewers.
10. Riewald lists uncollected items for this period, pp. 271-74, 288-89.
11. Riewald, p. 291, item 439, mistakenly attributes Turner's letter "An Unhappy Poet," September 19, 1896, to Beerbohm (see *Letters*, p. 110, fn. 3). Beerbohm's own unsigned article of September 12 is not listed. Beerbohm's review of Scott's essays, *Sisters by the Sea*, appeared September 4, 1897. When Scott died, Beerbohm published a tribute to him (*The Saturday Review*, July 2, 1904). Scott, he said, was unrivaled as a critic of acting, and though he was reactionary in the 1890's, he had served the theater well in earlier years.
12. The parodies quoted are reprinted in *Parodies: An Anthology from Chaucer to Beerbohm*, ed. Dwight MacDonald (London, 1961), pp. 201-9, 460-62. Other authors parodied in the series were the sentimental Scotch novelist Ian MacLaren, Alice Meynell, and George Meredith. The Meredith parody, revised, was included in *A Christmas Garland* (1912).
13. This review followed the article on Jerome in *The Daily Mail*, March 13, 1897. Beerbohm's uniformly unfavorable allusions to this popular humorist may result in part from Jerome's early objections to Oscar Wilde, whose contribution to *The Spirit Lamp* he had drawn attention to in *To-day*, December 29, 1894. See Frances Winwar, *Oscar Wilde and the Yellow Nineties*, p. 252.
14. "Some Words on Royalty," *Outlook*, February 12 and 19; "Aubrey Beardsley," *The Idler*, May; "Many Happy Returns," *London Life*, September 17. The esssay on Beardsley is discussed later in this chapter. The contribution to *London Life* takes its title from the fact that Beerbohm's birthday approximated the date of the founding of that magazine.
15. *Works* (London, 1896), p. 26.
16. "The Incomparable Beauty of Modern Dress," *Spirit Lamp*, June, 1893, pp. 90-98; "Dandies and Dandies," *Vanity* (New York), February 7, 14, 21, 28, 1895; "Notes on Foppery," *Unicorn* (London), September 18 and 25.
17. *The Incomparable Max*, ed. S. C. Roberts (London, 1962).
18. *More* (London, 1899), pp. 11, 26, 33, 44, 69, 107.
19. "Two Glimpses of Andrew Lang," *Life and Letters* (June, 1928), pp. 1-11.

20. Lewis Melville (Lewis S. Benjamin), *Not All the Truth* (London, 1928), p. 243.

21. *A Variety of Things* (London, 1928), pp. 309-53.

22. For an account of a recent unsuccessful dramatic version see *The New Yorker,* September 14, 1968, pp. 129-30.

23. *Up the Years from Bloomsbury* (Boston, 1927), pp. 185-88.

24. Cecil, p. 245. In 1907, at Portofino, Beerbohm met the Baroness von Hutten, with whom he had a mild flirtation. See *Letters,* pp. 175-76 and Cecil, pp. 281-83, 285-96.

25. "Mr. Beardsley's Fifty Drawings," *To-morrow* (January-June, 1897), pp. 28-35. "Aubrey Beardsley," *The Idler* (May, 1898), p. 539; reprinted in *A Variety of Things* (1928).

26. *The Saturday Review,* December 8, 1900, appended to the review of Louis N. Parker's *The Swashbuckler.* "A Lord of Language," *Vanity Fair,* March 2, 1905, p. 309.

27. *Yet Again* (London, 1909), p. 85.

28. Added in the Collected Edition.

29. Besides the nine "Words for Pictures" in *Yet Again,* there are several uncollected contributions of this kind: *The Saturday Review,* April 30, 1898 (two items), and August 13, 1898; and *The New Liberal Review,* July, 1901, two items.

Chapter Three

1. To simplify documentation of this chapter, the complete date will identify reviews still in the files of *The Saturday Review.* When the date is given by year only, the review is reprinted in *Around Theatres* (London, 1924). Published by William Heinemann as volumes VIII and IX of the *Collected Edition, Around Theatres* was separately issued in 1924. In 1930 Alfred A. Knopf published an American edition in two volumes, but with different pagination. In 1953 Rupert Hart-Davis, London, published a one-volume edition with still different pagination. This last is the text I have used. Since in all three editions the reviews are arranged chronologically, with the exact date given at the head of each, the specific review may readily be found. The 1953 edition indexes the plays reviewed. Riewald, pp. 333-43, gives a subject index to all the dramatic criticisms. For some brief quotations I have given page references to *Around Theatres* (1953), referred to as *Theatres.*

2. In the Shaw papers at the British Museum. The letter is virtually a first draft of Beerbohm's first article as staff critic, "Why I Ought Not to Have Become a Dramatic Critic," May 28. Frank Harris, "Max Beerbohm," *Contemporary Portraits: Fourth Series* (London, 1924), p. 131, blandly says that *he* asked Beerbohm to fill Shaw's place.

3. This is the first review in *Around Theatres.*

4. This is the last review in *Around Theatres.*

5. *Theatres,* pp. 92, 102, 186, 472: June 30, 1900; July 14, 1900; December 7, 1901; August 17, 1907.

6. *Our Theatres in the Nineties,* 3 vols. (London: Constable and Co., Ltd., 1948): preface, I, v. Originally published in the Standard Edition of Shaw in 1932. In 1906 James Huneker had edited a selection, *Dramatic Opinions and Essays.* "The Author's Apology" for the 1906 volume appears with a postscript dated 1931.

7. The Maugham plays reviewed were: *A Man of Honour,* February 28, 1903 and March 5, 1904; *Jack Straw,* April 4, 1904; and *The Explorer,* June 20, 1908.

8. *Mainly on the Air* (London, 1957), pp. 95-101.

9. Uncollected articles dealing with Shakespeare appeared in *The Saturday Review* as follows: "Oxford Revisited," *A Midsummer Night's Dream,* February 18, 1899; "The Ghetto and Other Plays," *Richard III,* September 16, 1899; "*King John* and Other Plays," September 30, 1899; "At Her Majesty's," *A Midsummer Night's Dream,* January 20, 1900; "At the Lyceum," *Richard II* and *Twelfth Night,* March 24, 1900; "Acting Good and Evil," *Antony and Cleopatra,* April 7, 1900; "Caesar and Cromwell," *Julius Caesar,* September 15, 1900; "Shakespeare in Two Directions," *Henry V* and *The Taming of the Shrew,* January 5, 1901; *The Merchant of Venice,* January 19, 1901; *Twelfth Night,* February 9, 1901; "*Hamlet* in Panton Street," March 30, 1901; *Coriolanus,* April 27, 1901; "Several Theatres," *Much Ado About Nothing,* June 1, 1901; "The Lyric, the Garrick, and the O.U.D.S.," *The Two Gentlemen of Verona,* February 15, 1902; "A New Play and an Old," *The Merry Wives of Windsor,* June 14, 1902; "*Hamlet* and the Hedonists," July 12, 1902; "*Othello* Reinterpreted," December 20, 1902; "*Much Ado* and Mr. Craig's Setting," May 30, 1903; "Brutus as Villain," *Julius Caesar,* February 17, 1906; "Brutus: Villain or Hero," *Julius Caesar,* February 24, 1906; "O.U.D.S.," *A Midsummer Night's Dream,* February 29, 1908; "Tickled Groundlings," *Romeo and Juliet,* March 21, 1908; "*Lear* at the Haymarket," September 18, 1909.

Chapter Four

1. Details of Villino Chiaro are drawn chiefly from Behrman, pp. 39-41, 222; and from Cecil, pp. 39-41, 91, 222, 304-6. Beerbohm's sketch is reproduced in *Letters,* p. 189.

2. Cecil, p. 306.

3. *Letters,* pp. 187, 199, 221; Cecil, p. 331.

4. *Letters,* pp. 234-39.

5. Rothenstein, II, 312-15.

6. *Letters,* p. 273.

7. *The Daily Herald,* May 18, 1921, p. 1. Quoted by Cecil, pp. 387-88.

8. Behrman, p. 79, gives a complete transcription of the caption.

9. Cecil, p. 399.

10. Sydney Schiff, under the pseudonym of Stephen Hudson, published several novels.

11. Rothenstein, III, 129, 142.

12. See the favorable notice by a friend of Beerbohm in *The New Statesman and Nation,* May 16, 1931, pp. 425-26.

13. Reprinted in *Mainly on the Air* (1946).

14. Cecil, pp. 430-32.

15. From the printed address; copies at Merton College, Oxford, and at the Huntington Library.

16. Cecil, pp. 453-54.

17. Behrman, p. 124.

18. Henry James's "The Velvet Glove" appeared in *The English Review* in March, 1909, not in 1906, as Beerbohm states.

19. Behrman, pp. 14, 26-29. The Henderson volume is now in the Berg Collection of the New York Public Library.

20. Behrman, p. 71.

21. Behrman, pp. 231-32. Gosse's letter, passing on James's favorable comments, is quoted from Evan Charteris, *The Life and Letters of Sir Edmund Gosse* (London, 1931), pp. 350-51.

22. Behrman, p. 298.

23. Cecil, p. 495.

Chapter Five

1. *Letters,* p. 143. *Theatres,* pp. 224-25. *The Adventures of Mr. Verdant Green,* by Cuthbert Bede (pseudonym of Edward Bradley), appeared in 1853. Bradley, it is necessary to state, was a graduate of Durham; and there is some reason to doubt whether he was ever in Oxford. The novel was popular for years and was even dramatized.

2. *Zuleika Dobson* (London, 1911), pp. 64 (ch. v), 87 (ch. vi), 90 (ch. vii).

3. *Letters,* pp. 53, 72.

4. Riewald, p. 125, insists that *Zuleika Dobson* is not a novel but a fantasy.

5. *A Christmas Garland* (London, 1912), p. 3.

6. Pp. 125, 129, 159, 192. Conrad in *Prefaces* (London, 1937), p. 58, comments good-naturedly on this parody of "The Lagoon."

7. *The Saturday Review,* June 18, 1904; *Theatres,* pp. 373-76.

8. *The Saturday Review,* December 8, 1906.
9. *Seven Men and Two Others* (London, 1950), pp. 243-44.
10. Cecil, p. 295.
11. *A Variety of Things* (London, 1928), p. 86.
12. Gerald Gould, *The Saturday Review,* November 17, 1928, pp. 645-46.
13. Riewald, p. 79.
14. *The Mirror of the Past* is mentioned at the end of "Hethway Speaking," *Mainly on the Air* (New York, 1958), p. 130.
15. *And Even Now* (London, 1920), p. 233.

Chapter Six

1. *Theatres,* pp. 65, 109.
2. First appeared in *The Daily Mail,* January 16, 1897. Reprinted in *More* (1899).
3. First appeared in *Pall Mall Magazine* (January-April, 1901). Reprinted in *A Variety of Things* (1928).
4. Cecil, p. 411.
5. Bernard Falk, *Thomas Rowlandson: His Life and Art* (London, 1949).
6. Bohun Lynch, *Max in Perspective* (London, 1921), p. 106, reproduced six of these drawings. Alan Dent, "Caricatures from Max Beerbohm's Schoolboy Notebooks," *John o' London's Weekly,* April 1, 1949, reproduced twelve.
7. "When I Was Nineteen," *Strand,* CXII (October, 1946), 51-55. Fifteen of the original drawings are reproduced.
8. *The Strand,* IX (January, 1895), 109-15. "Harold George" is a pseudonym for John Harold Marston and George Ronald Wood, contemporaries of Max at Merton. See *Letters,* p. 56, fn. 1.
9. *Max's Nineties: Drawings 1892-1899* (London, 1958).
10. *Letters,* p. 129.
11. *Letters,* pp. 97, 201.
12. *Letters,* pp. 201, 226, 256.
13. Riewald, p. 31.
14. The drawing is in the Thomas Hardy Collection in the Dorset County Museum, Dorchester.

Chapter Seven

1. Cecil, p. 491.
2. Bohun Lynch, *Max in Perspective* (London, 1921). The letter is given in full in the introductory pages.

3. *The Saturday Review,* October 27, 1900.
4. *Spectator,* November 5, 1943, p. 432.
5. Riewald, pp. 206-11.
6. *And Even Now* (London, 1920), pp. 303-4. The essay was first published in this volume.
7. Rothenstein, III, p. 82.
8. *Mainly on the Air* (London, 1957), p. 174.
9. Cecil, pp. 413-40; Behrman, p. 19. For details of editions and sales, see Riewald, pp. 233-55.
10. B. R. McElderry, Jr., "Beerbohm on Trollope," *London Times Literary Supplement,* October 12, 1967, p. 968.
11. *The Saturday Review,* July 22, 1905.
12. Rothenstein, II, 314.

Selected Bibliography

GALLATIN, A. E. *Sir Max Beerbohm: Bibliographical Notes.* Cambridge, Mass.: Harvard University Press, 1944. A catalogue of Mr. Gallatin's own collection, now at the Houghton Library, Harvard University. The list of "Uncollected and Unpublished Caricatures" is particularly useful. On pp. 103-12 Beerbohm's drawings for the stage version of *The Happy Hypocrite,* and drawings of Turner, Wilde, Whistler, and Edward VII, are reproduced.

GALLATIN, A. E. and L. M. OLIVER. *A Bibliography of the Works of Max Beerbohm.* Cambridge, Mass.: Harvard University Press, 1952. In part a revision of Gallatin's *Notes* (1944), but confined to the collected and separately printed works.

RIEWALD, J. G. *Sir Max Beerbohm Man and Writer: A Critical Analysis with a Brief Life and a Bibliography.* The Hague: Martinus Nijhoff, 1953. This indispensable volume devotes pp. 1-31 to biography, pp. 31-212 to critical analysis, and pp. 213-333 to a detailed bibliography. All editions of Beerbohm's books are listed, as well as more than four hundred uncollected magazine contributions, and three hundred books and articles including critical opinion. Riewald lists collections of caricatures but does not deal with the many scattered drawings, published and unpublished. The book was later issued by the Stephen Greene Press, Brattleboro, Vermont.

Primary Sources

1. Collections of Beerbohmiana

Charterhouse (Godalming, Sussex)

The school library has, besides the principal published volumes, framed caricatures of Charterhouse masters; several later caricatures, including one of Edward VII; a verse manuscript, "The Epic of Hades," by a schoolmate, with some thirty illustrations by Beerbohm; the Minute Book of the Charterhouse Society, with some twenty Beerbohm drawings; exercise sheets with drawings of schoolmates and political figures; the manuscript of "Old Carthusian Memories," published in the school magazine and later reprinted in *A Variety of Things* (1928); copies of school magazines to which Beerbohm contributed; and copies of various articles about him.

Merton College, Oxford

The library has in its special Beerbohm Collection various documents such as certificates of birth, baptism, and marriage; the

Birthday Book, with personal messages from many literary men on Beerbohm's eightieth birthday; some forty volumes from his personal library, many "improved" with caricatures and marginalia; the blue oval doorplate of his study; his unpainted drawing table, designed so that he could stand while drawing; various caricatures and manuscripts; and a considerable number of letters, including a group written to the Sydney Schiffs in later years. There is a typed catalogue of the collection.

Ashmolean Museum, Oxford

From the collection of Philip Guedalla, the Museum received some sixty original caricatures. Several of these are reproduced in a souvenir booklet, listed in the Bibliography.

The British Museum, London

The Manuscript Room has a number of letters to Shaw, Edmund Gosse, and William Archer.

The Houghton Library, Harvard University

The library has the Gallatin Collection, described in the bibliographies above. Included are some twenty original drawings; several volumes with marginalia by Beerbohm; also letters to Reggie Turner and to William Rothenstein.

The Berg Collection, New York Public Library

Included are the "improved" copy of Henderson's biography of Shaw; a notebook with jottings on Henry James, Shaw, Gladstone, Churchill, and Edmund Gosse; a number of caricatures, and several letters.

The University of California at Los Angeles

The Majl Ewing Collection in the William Andrews Clark Library includes some forty drawings, first editions of the writings, several letters, manuscripts, and association items.

2. Writings

And Even Now. London: William Heinemann, 1920.

Around Theatres. 2 vols. London: William Heinemann, 1924. Also New York: Alfred A. Knopf, 1930. One-volume edition, London: Rupert Hart-Davis, 1953. "Beerbohm on Trollope," London *Times Literary Supplement,* October 12, 1967, p. 968. Hitherto unpublished letter, ed. B. R. McElderry, Jr.

A Christmas Garland. London: William Heinemann, 1912. An edition by the same publisher, 1950, added a parody of Maurice Baring.

The Happy Hypocrite. London: John Lane, 1897. This story was first published in *The Yellow Book,* October, 1896. It was reprinted in the first edition of *A Variety of Things* (1928), but omitted from the American edition and from later English editions. It is reprinted in Stanley Weintraub's selections from *The Yellow Book* (New York: Doubleday & Co., 1964).

Herbert Beerbohm Tree: Some Memories of Him and His Art. Ed. Max Beerbohm. London: Hutchinson & Co., 1920.

Leaves from the Garland. New York, 1926. Privately printed and unauthorized. Reprints six parodies from *The Saturday Review* of 1896.

Letters to Reggie Turner. Ed. Rupert Hart-Davis. London: Rupert Hart-Davis, 1964. Fully annotated. Reprints Beerbohm's article on Wilde (1893), his tribute to Dora (1940), a newspaper interview (1900); and publishes for the first time "The Maison Lefevre," a manuscript reminiscence of Dieppe.

Lytton Strachey. Cambridge University Press, 1943. Included in *Mainly on the Air* (London: William Heinemann, 1957 and New York: Alfred A. Knopf, 1958); also in S. C. Roberts, *The Incomparable Max* (London: William Heinemann, 1962).

Mainly on the Air. London: William Heinemann, 1946. A later edition, same publisher, 1957, added eight radio talks and the lecture, *Lytton Strachey.*

The Incomparable Max. A Selection introduced by S. C. Roberts. London: William Heinemann, 1962. Among thirty-three items included are "From a Brother's Standpoint," from the memorial volume for Herbert Beerbohm Tree, and the lecture on Lytton Strachey.

Max in Verse. Collected and annotated by J. G. Riewald. Brattleboro, Vermont: The Stephen Greene Press, 1963. Includes 84 items, 34 of them previously unpublished.

More. London: John Lane, 1899.

More Theatres: 1898-1903. London: Rupert Hart-Davis, 1969.

A Peep Into the Past. New York: [Max Harzof], 1923. This satire on Oscar Wilde was privately printed, and unauthorized.

Seven Men. London: William Heinemann, 1919. An enlarged edition entitled *Seven Men and Two Others,* by the same publisher, 1950, included "Felix Argallo and Walter Ledgett." This sketch first appeared in *The London Mercury,* May, 1927, as "Not That I Would Boast," and under this title was included in the first edition of *A Variety of Things* (1928).

A Variety of Things. London: William Heinemann, 1928. "Not That I Would Boast" and "The Happy Hypocrite" were dropped from the American edition and from later English editions.

The Works of Max Beerbohm with a Bibliography by John Lane. London: John Lane, 1896.

The Works of Max Beerbohm. 10 vols. London: William Heinemann, 1922-1928. *The Works; More; Yet Again; And Even Now; A Christ-*

mas Garland; Zuleika Dobson; Seven Men; Around Theatres (vols. eight and nine); *A Variety of Things.*

Yet Again. London: Chapman and Hall, 1909.

Zuleika Dobson. London: William Heinemann, 1911.

3. Drawings

A Book of Caricatures. London: Methuen & Co., 1907. Includes 48 numbered drawings and a frontispiece.

Caricatures by Max. Oxford University Press, 1958. Reproduces 28 drawings from the Guedalla collection at the Ashmolean Museum.

Caricatures of Twenty-five Gentlemen. London: Leonard Smithers, 1896.

Cartoons: "The Second Childhood of John Bull." London: Stephen Swift & Co. Ltd., 1911. Fifteen unnumbered drawings.

Fifty Caricatures. London: William Heinemann, 1913.

Heroes and Heroines of Bitter Sweet. London: Messrs. Leadlay, Ltd., 1931.

Max's Nineties. London: Rupert Hart-Davis, 1958. Includes 46 caricatures, many hitherto uncollected from magazines in which they appeared, and the previously unpublished series of eleven on Gladstone.

Observations. London: William Heinemann, 1925. Includes 51 numbered caricatures and a frontispiece.

The Poets' Corner. London: William Heinemann, 1904. Includes 20 drawings in color. Also published, with an introduction by John Rothenstein, and with four drawings from *Rossetti and His Circle* (London: King Penguin Books, 1943).

Rossetti and His Circle. London: William Heinemann, 1922. Includes 22 drawings plus a frontispiece, all in color.

A Survey. London: William Heinemann, 1921. Includes 51 tinted caricatures, plus frontispiece.

Things New and Old. London: William Heinemann, 1923. Includes 49 numbered caricatures, plus frontispiece.

Secondary Sources

Ashbee, C. R. *Caricature.* London: Chapman and Hall, Ltd., 1928. Useful survey; includes four drawings by Beerbohm.

Behrman, S. N. *Portrait of Max.* New York: Random House, 1960. First appeared as a series of seven articles in *The New Yorker,* February 6 to March 19, 1960. Informal and anecdotal, but perceptive and precise. About forty excellent illustrations.

BICKLEY, FRANCIS LAWRANCE. *The Pre-Raphaelite Comedy*. London: Constable & Co., Ltd., 1932. Chiefly concerned with the nature and impact of the paintings.

BURDETT, OSBERT. *The Beardsley Period.* London: John Lane, 1925. Sympathetic treatment of sources and influences.

CECIL, DAVID. *Max, A Biography*. London: Constable, 1964. Before Beerbohm died he expressed a wish that Cecil write his biography, if one was desired. Cecil drew largely on *Letters to Reggie Turner* (1964), on many unpublished letters, and other contemporary sources, but gives little documentation. About thirty illustrations.

ENSOR, R. C. K. *England 1870-1914*. Oxford: Clarendon Press, 1936. Standard.

FELSTINER, JOHN. "Max Beerbohm and the Wings of Henry James," *Kenyon Review,* XXIX (September, 1967), 449-71. Emphasizes Beerbohm's skill as parodist.

JACKSON, HOLBROOK. *The Eighteen-Nineties: A Review of the Art and Ideas at the Close of the Nineteenth Century*. London: Grant Richards, 1913. Dedicated to Beerbohm and praised by him.

LE GALLIENNE, RICHARD. *The Romantic 90's*. London and New York: G. P. Putnam's Sons, 1926. Reminiscences by a minor author of the period.

LYNCH, [JOHN GILBERT] BOHUN. *Max in Perspective*. London: William Heinemann, 1922. The first book-length account, by an appreciative younger friend, himself a caricaturist and essayist.

MACDONALD, DWIGHT. *Parodies: An Anthology from Chaucer to Beerbohm — And After*. London: Faber and Faber, 1960. Excellent introductory comment. Ten parodies by Beerbohm are included.

MCELDERRY, B. R., JR. "Max Beerbohm: Essayist, Caricaturist, Novelist," *On Stage and Off: Eight Essays in English Literature,* pp. 76-86. Washington State University Press, 1968. Brief evaluation.

MAY, J. LEWIS. *John Lane and the Nineties*. London: John Lane, 1936. Account of Lane's activities as publisher and as friend of Beerbohm, Rothenstein, and many others.

MIX, KATHERINE LYON. *A Study in Yellow: The Yellow Book and Its Contributors*. Lawrence: University of Kansas Press, 1960. Thorough study; especially useful for minor figures.

MOERS, ELLEN. *The Dandy: Brummell to Beerbohm*. London: Secker and Warburg, 1960. Emphasizes Beerbohm's early essays.

ROBERTS, S. C. *Zuleika in Cambridge*. Cambridge: W. Heffer & Sons, Ltd., 1941. Brief, witty sequel to *Zuleika Dobson;* praised by Beerbohm.

ROSS, MARGERY. *Robert Ross: Friend of Friends*. London: Cape, 1952. Most comprehensive account of Wilde's friend and literary executor.

ROTHENSTEIN, WILLIAM. *Men and Memories: 1872-1900; Men and Memories: 1900-1922; Since Fifty: Men and Memories 1922-1938*. New York: Coward McCann, 1931, 1932, 1939. This three-volume work is the most valuable single source for literary and artistic activities related to Beerbohm's career.

SHAW, G. B. *Our Theatres in the Nineties*. 3 vols. London: Constable and Co., Ltd., 1948. Collection of Shaw's dramatic criticism in *The Saturday Review*, 1895-1898.

SPEAIGHT, ROBERT. *William Rothenstein*. London: Ellis & Spottiswoode, 1962. Summarizes and supplements Rothenstein's extensive memoirs, cited above.

SWINNERTON, FRANK. *The Georgian Literary Scene*. London: J. M. Dent & Sons, Ltd. 1938. As author and publisher, Swinnerton knew Beerbohm and many of his friends.

TAYLOR, A. J. P. *English History 1914-1945*. Oxford: Oxford University Press. 1965. Standard.

THORPE, JAMES. *English Illustration:* The Nineties. London: Faber and Faber, 1935. Comprehensive account of magazine art and artists.

WARD, LESLIE. *Forty Years of "Spy."* London: Chatto and Windus, 1915. Reminiscences by the cartoonist for *Vanity Fair*. Illustrated.

WEINTRAUB, STANLEY. *The Yellow Book: Quintessence of the Nineties*. New York: Doubleday & Co., Inc., 1964. Convenient anthology, with brief introduction. Includes Beerbohm's "A Defence of Cosmetics," "1880," and "The Happy Hypocrite."

———.*Reggie: Portrait of Reginald Turner*. New York: George Braziller, 1965. Biography of Beerbohm's close friend from 1890 until Turner's death in 1938.

———. *The Savoy: Nineties Experiment*. Philadelphia: University of Pennsylvania Press, 1966. Includes Beerbohm's "A Good Prince," several Beardsley illustrations, and the tables of contents for the eight issues of *The Savoy*, all published in 1896.

———.*Beardsley: A Biography*. New York: George Braziller, 1967. Detailed examination of Beardsley's brief career.

WILDE, OSCAR. *The Letters of Oscar Wilde*. Ed. Rupert Hart-Davis. London: Rupert Hart-Davis, 1962. Following many fragmentary and misleading publications of Wilde's letters, this edition is definitive.

WINWAR, FRANCES (Mrs Bernard Grebanier). *Oscar Wilde and the Yellow Nineties*. New York: Harper, 1940. Lively, detailed popular account.

Index

(The works of Max Beerbohm, divided into caricatures and literary sections, are listed under his name)

WITHDRAWN